CLASSIC BATTLES

IWO JIMA 1945

THE MARINES RAISE THE FLAG
ON MOUNT SURIBACHI

TEXT BY
DERRICK WRIGHT

BATTLESCENE PLATES BY
JIM LAURIER

First published in Great Britain in 2001 by Osprey Publishing, Elms Court, Chapel Way, Botley, Oxford OX2 9LP, United Kingdom.
Email: info@ospreypublishing.com

ISBN 1 84176 374 8

Editor: Chris Wheatley
Design: The Black Spot
Indexing: Alan Rutter
Origination by Grasmere Digital Imaging Ltd, Leeds, UK
Printed in China through World Print Ltd.

01 02 03 04 05   10 9 8 7 6 5 4 3 2 1

For a catalog of all books published by Osprey Military and Aviation please contact:

The Marketing Manager, Osprey Direct UK, PO Box 140, Wellingborough, Northants, NN8 4ZA, United Kingdom.
Tel. +44 (0)1933 443863, Fax +44 (0)1933 443849.
Email: info@ospreydirect.co.uk

The Marketing Manager, Osprey Direct USA, c/o Motorbooks International, PO Box 1, Osceola, WI 54020-0001, USA.
Email: info@ospreydirectusa.com

Buy online at www.ospreypublishing.com

Author's Note

The author wishes to thank Mr. Taro Kuribayashi, son of the commander of the Iwo Jima garrison LtGen Tadamichi Kuribayashi, for permission to quote from his father's writings and for supplying photographs from the family collection.

Thanks also to Mr. Joe Rosenthal for a definitive account of the famous flag raising on Mount Suribachi and to General Paul Tibbets for information and photograph.

Other photographs are from the National Archives Washington, DC, USMC, US Navy, US Air Force or as credited in the text.

Editor's Note

Many thanks are due to Jim Moran for his invaluable help in supplying references for the battlescenes and bird's-eye-views which appear in this book.

KEY TO MILITARY SYMBOLS

PAGE 2 **Marines of G Company 24th Regiment. (USMC)**

PAGE 3 **Marines utilize a captured Japanese Nambo machine gun. (National Archives)**

CONTENTS

ORIGINS OF THE CAMPAIGN

As the final days of 1944 ebbed away the Japanese were facing defeat on all fronts. The heady days of conquest that had followed the attack on Pearl Harbor on December 7, 1941, and the occupation of the Philippines, Singapore, Hong Kong, and the oil rich Dutch East Indies, were little more than a memory as they prepared to defend the homeland at the inner limits of their defensive perimeter.

After suffering staggering defeats at Midway, the Philippine Sea and Leyte Gulf, the Imperial Navy was impotent in the face of the massive US Task Forces that scoured the Pacific and accompanied every amphibious landing.

In the west, British and Commonwealth forces of the 14th Army had pushed the enemy back from the borders of India, and in bitter fighting in some of the worst jungle terrain in the world were driving the Japanese Army along the Irrawaddy River into central Burma.

RIGHT **A flight of B29s head for North Field on Guam after returning from another fire raising attack on the Japanese mainland. (National Archives)**

LEFT **Four Grumman Avenger torpedo-bombers unload their bombs in the area between Airfields Nos. 1 & 2. The cliffs of the Quarry overlooking the East Boat Basin can be seen in the foreground. (National Archives)**

7

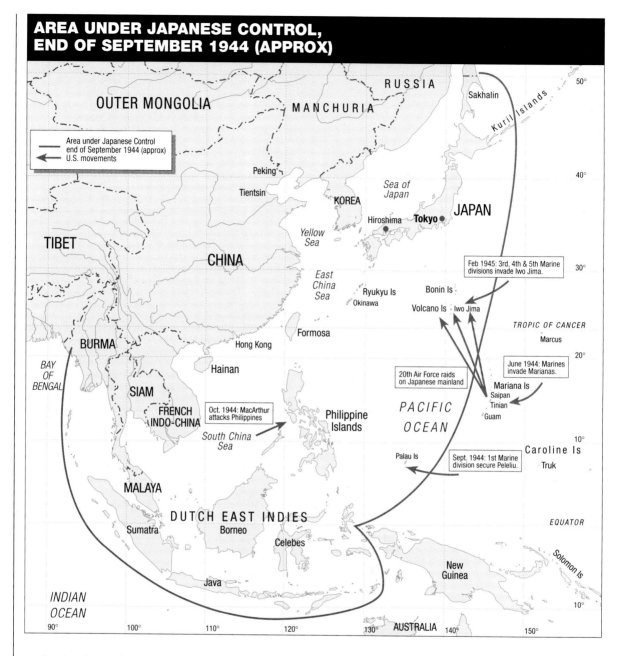

AREA UNDER JAPANESE CONTROL, END OF SEPTEMBER 1944 (APPROX)

Area under Japanese Control end of September 1944 (approx)
U.S. movements

RUSSIA

OUTER MONGOLIA

MANCHURIA

Sakhalin

Kuril Islands

50°

40°

Peking

Tientsin

KOREA

Sea of Japan

Hiroshima · **Tokyo** ● JAPAN

TIBET

CHINA

Yellow Sea

East China Sea

Feb 1945: 3rd, 4th & 5th Marine divisions invade Iwo Jima.

30°

Ryukyu Is
Okinawa

Bonin Is

Volcano Is Iwo Jima

TROPIC OF CANCER

Marcus

BURMA

Formosa

Hong Kong

20°

BAY OF BENGAL

Hainan

20th Air Force raids on Japanese mainland

June 1944: Marines invade Marianas.

SIAM

FRENCH INDO-CHINA

Oct. 1944: MacArthur attacks Philippines

Philippine Islands

PACIFIC OCEAN

Mariana Is
Saipan
Tinian
Guam

South China Sea

10°

Caroline Is

Palau Is

Sept. 1944: 1st Marine division secure Peleliu.

Truk

MALAYA

DUTCH EAST INDIES

Sumatra   Borneo

Celebes

EQUATOR

New Guinea

Solomon Is

INDIAN OCEAN

Java

10°

90°   100°   110°   120°   130° AUSTRALIA 140°   150°

In the Central Pacific, Gen MacArthur's army had advanced through the Solomons and across New Guinea and by October, 1944, had invaded Leyte in the Philippines, redeeming his pledge that "I shall return." Through the islands and atolls to the north, Adm Nimitz's Marines swept onward in their "island hopping" campaign that had begun at Tarawa in 1943 and was to climax at Okinawa in 1945. Seizing only those islands that were essential for the support of further operations and bypassing and neutralizing the others, the Marines had by August, 1944, occupied the main islands of the Marianas – Guam, Saipan and Tinian.

The unique strategic location of Iwo Jima, midway along the B29 Superfortress route from the Marianas to Tokyo, made it imperative

ABOVE **The B29 Superfortress bomber was the most advanced aircraft of its day. With pressurized crew compartments, remote control gun turrets, a huge range and bomb load, it was able to reach the Japanese mainland with ease. Here, rows of brand new aircraft stand outside of the plant specially constructed for the B29 program at Wichita, Kansas. (Boeing Company Archives)**

that the island should come under American control. Prior to the occupation of Saipan, Tinian and Guam, the B29s had been limited to carrying out raids on southern Japan from bases in central China. With the problem of transporting all of their fuel by air over thousands of miles of inhospitable country and the limitations of small bomb loads, the attacks had little impact. But now, with the construction of five huge airfields 1,500 miles from the Japanese mainland, the way was open for the 20th Air Force to mount a massive campaign against the industrial heartland of Japan.

Initially the 20th Air Force had attempted to duplicate the technique which had been so successfully used by the 8th Air Force in their bombing campaign against Germany – daylight precision bombing. The experiment had failed largely because of unexpectedly high winds as the Superfortresses approached their targets at altitudes of 27,000–33,000ft in the jetstream. The Air Force commander, BrigGen Haywood Hansell, became increasingly frustrated and blamed his crews for the disappointing results; and by January, 1945, the chiefs in Washington had decided that Hansell had to go.

His replacement was Curtis LeMay, a brilliant technician who had previously been in command of the 3rd Division of the 8th Air Force in England. LeMay was to introduce a new term to the aircrews of the 20th Air Force – "area bombing." Widely used by the RAF throughout the war, he proposed to firebomb the main cities of Japan at low level and by night in a dramatic reversal of Hansell's earlier tactics. LeMay was aware that his career was on the line. He had not informed Gen Henry "Hap" Arnold, Commanding General of the Air Force, of this first low altitude raid: "If we go in low, at night, not in formation, I think we'll surprise the Japs, at least for a short period. If it's a failure and I don't produce any results then he can fire me," he said.

The only obstacle on the flight path was Iwo Jima. It housed two airfields with a third under construction, and a radar station that could

Once their airfields became operational in the Mariana Islands, the B29 bombers began a relentless campaign against the Japanese mainland. Here, a group of B29s passes over one of Japan's most famous landmarks, Mount Fujiyama, on their way to Tokyo. (National Archives)

give two hours warning of an impending raid. The Air Force desperately needed to eliminate the threat of fighter attacks from the Iwo airfields and to neutralize the radar station there. With the island under American control there would be the added bonuses of a refuge for crippled bombers, facilities for air-sea rescue flying boats, and more importantly, a base from which P51 Mustang long range fighters could escort the Superfortresses on the second leg of their long haul to Japan.

At Iwo Jima the amphibious techniques which had been developed over the previous three years were to receive the supreme test as three Marine divisions pitted themselves against more than 21,000 deeply entrenched Japanese troops led by a brilliant and determined commander, LtGen Tadamichi Kuribayashi. "Do not plan for my return," he was to inform his wife from Iwo Jima. Sadly his words would also be the epitaph for nearly 6,000 US Marines.

Lieutenant-General "Howlin' Mad" Smith, Commander Fleet Marine Forces Pacific, called the battle: "The most savage and most costly battle in the history of the Marine Corps." Smith had fronted every amphibious landing in the Central Pacific from Tarawa in 1943 to the Marianas in late 1944 and was eminently qualified to make such a judgment. As the battle reached its climax, Adm Chester Nimitz was to add his now famous phrase: "Among the Americans who fought on Iwo Jima, uncommon valor was a common virtue."

OPPOSING COMMANDERS

Fleet Admiral Chester Nimitz was appointed Commander in Chief Pacific (CICPAC) after the Pearl Harbor debacle. A great organizer and leader, he was by the end of 1945 the commander of the largest military force ever, overseeing 21 admirals and generals, 6 Marine divisions, 5,000 aircraft, and the world's largest navy. (US Navy)

AMERICAN

On October 3, 1944, the joint Chiefs of Staff issued a directive to Adm CHESTER NIMITZ, Commander in Chief Pacific (CINCPAC) to occupy the island of Iwo Jima. As with previous amphibious landings in the Marine Corps "island hopping" campaign, he entrusted the planning and implementation of the assault, codenamed "Operation Detachment," to his experienced trio of tacticians, Spruance, Turner, and Smith who had masterminded almost every operation since the initial landing at Tarawa in 1943.

Nimitz was a quiet somewhat introverted Texan who never lost a sea battle. President Roosevelt had been so impressed by him that he bypassed nearly thirty more senior admirals to appoint him CINCPAC after the removal of Adm Husband E. Kimmel following the debacle at Pearl Harbor. One of his greatest abilities was to resolve conflicts with other senior officers. However, his long running disputes with Gen Douglas MacArthur, Supreme Commander of all US Army units in the Pacific Theatre, were legendary. A man of striking contrasts, MacArthur was arrogant, conceited, egotistical, and flamboyant and yet a superb strategist with an amazing sense of where and when to strike the enemy to greatest advantage.

Nimitz and MacArthur disagreed throughout the war on the best way to defeat the Japanese, with MacArthur favoring a thrust through the Philippines and on to Formosa (Taiwan) and China. Nimitz stood by his "island hopping" theory – occupying those islands and atolls that were of strategic importance and bypassing those that had little military value or were unsuitable for amphibious landings.

Admiral RAYMOND A. SPRUANCE had been Nimitz's right hand man since his outstanding performance at the Battle of Midway in June, 1942. His quiet unassuming manner concealed a razor sharp intellect and an ability to utilize the experience and knowledge of his staff to a remarkable degree. He would continue in the role of Operations Commander until the final battle of the Pacific War at Okinawa.

Admiral RICHMOND KELLY TURNER, the Joint Expeditionary Force Commander, was by contrast notorious for his short temper and foul mouth, but his amazing organization skills placed him in a unique position to mount the operation. Dovetailing the dozens of air strikes and shore bombardments, disembarking thousands of troops and landing them on the right beach in the right sequence was an awesome responsibility fraught with the seeds of potential disaster, but Turner had proved his ability time and time again.

Lieutenant-General HOLLAND M. SMITH, Commanding General Fleet Marine Force Pacific, "Howlin' Mad" Smith to his Marines, was on

ABOVE, LEFT **Admiral Raymond Spruance was selected by Adm "Bull" Halsey as his own replacement before the Battle of Midway when Halsey was forced into hospital with dermatitis. His outstanding qualities soon attracted the attention of Nimitz who retained him as his Operations Commander for the remainder of the war. (National Archives)**

ABOVE, CENTRE
The acknowledged master of amphibious warfare, Kelly Turner's organizing skills were legendary. With the exception of Peleliu, he masterminded every landing in the Pacific from Guadalcanal to the final battle at Okinawa. (US Navy)

RIGHT **Lieutenant-General Holland M. Smith, "Howlin' Mad" to his Marines, was a volatile leader who did not suffer fools gladly. His dismissal of Army Gen Ralph Smith during the Saipan operation was to cause friction between the Army and the Marines for years. Seen here in two-toned helmet alongside Secretary of the Navy James Forrestal (with binoculars) and a group of Iwo Jima Marines. (National Archives)**

the other hand nearing the end of his active career. His aggressive tactics and uncompromising attitude had made him many enemies. In America a powerful clique of publishing barons was running a vitriolic campaign against him in favor of Gen Douglas MacArthur, and his recent dismissal of the Army's Gen Ralph Smith during the Saipan battle for "lack of aggressiveness" had not endeared him to the top brass in the Pentagon. At Iwo Jima he was content to keep a low profile in favor of MajGen Harry Schmidt, V Amphibious Corps Commander: "I think that they only asked me along in case anything happened to Harry Schmidt," he was to say after the battle.

The Iwo Jima landing would involve an unprecedented assembly of three Marine divisions: the 3rd, 4th and 5th. Heading the 3rd Division was MajGeneral GRAVES B. ERSKINE, at 47 a veteran of the battles of Belleau Wood, Chateau Thierry, and St Mihiel during World War I. Later

OPPOSITE, RIGHT **Forty-three year old MajGen Graves B. Erskine had commanded the 3rd Division since they captured Guam. Tough on discipline, he was well respected by his men who nicknamed him "The Big E." (Marine Corps Historical Collection)**

ABOVE, LEFT **A World War I veteran, MajGen Clifton B. Cates was outstanding at Iwo Jima. He continued a distinguished career in the Marine Corps to become Commandant in 1948. (National Archives)**

ABOVE, CENTRE **Seeing action for the first time, the 5th Division was to be commanded by the conqueror of Roi-Namur, Saipan and Tinian, MajGen Keller E. Rockey, another World War I veteran. (National Archives)**

ABOVE, RIGHT **"The Dutchman," MajGen Harry Schmidt, was to command V Amphibious Corps, the largest force the Marine Corps had ever put in the field. A veteran of numerous inter-war actions ranging from China to Nicaragua, he was 58 years old at the time of the battle. (US Marine Corps)**

he was the Chief of Staff to Holland Smith during the campaigns in the Aleutians, Gilbert Islands and the Marianas.

The 4th Division was also commanded by a World War I veteran, MajGen CLIFTON B. CATES, who had won the Navy Cross and two Silver Stars. At Guadalcanal in 1942 he had commanded the 4th Division's 1st Regiment and at Tinian became the Divisional Commander. In 1948 he became the Commandant of the Marine Corps.

Major-General KELLER E. ROCKEY was another Navy Cross holder for gallantry at Chateau Thierry. He won a second Navy Cross for heroism in Nicaragua in the inter-war years and took command of the 5th Division in February, 1944. Iwo Jima was to be the Division's first battle but it boasted a strong nucleus of veterans of the recently disbanded Raider Battalions and Marine Paratroopers.

Responsibility for preparing and executing Marine operations for "Detachment" fell to V Amphibious Corps Landing Force Commander MajGen HARRY SCHMIDT. A veteran of pre-war actions in China, the Philippines, Mexico, Cuba and Nicaragua and later the 4th Division commander during the Roi-Namur and Saipan invasions, he was 58 years old at Iwo Jima and would have the honour of fronting the largest Marine Corps force ever committed to a single battle.

JAPANESE

In May, LtGen TADAMICHI KURIBAYASHI had been summoned to the office of the Japanese Prime Minister, General Tojo, and told that he would be the commander of the garrison on Iwo Jima. Whether by accident or design the appointment proved to be a stroke of genius.

Kuribayashi, a samurai and long serving officer with 30 years distinguished service, had spent time in the United States as a deputy attaché and had proclaimed to his family: "the United States is the last country in the world that Japan should fight." He looked upon his appointment as both a challenge and a death sentence. "Do not plan for my return," he wrote to his wife shortly after his arrival on the island.

Kuribayashi succeeded in doing what no other Japanese commander in the Pacific could do – inflict more casualties on the US Marines than

his own troops suffered. Fifty-four years old at the time of the battle and quite tall for a Japanese at 5ft 9ins, Radio Tokyo described him as having the "traditional pot belly of a Samurai warrior and the heart of a Tiger."

Lieutenant-General Holland Smith in his memoirs was lavish in his praise for the commander's ability: "His ground organization was far superior to any I had seen in France in WWI and observers say it excelled the German ground organization in WWII. The only way we could move was behind rolling artillery barrages that pulverized the area and then we went in and reduced each position with flamethrowers, grenades and demolition charges. Some of his mortar and rocket launchers were cleverly hidden. We learned about them the hard way, through sickeningly heavy casualties. Every cave, every pillbox, every bunker was an individual battle where Marines and Japanese fought hand to hand to the death."

OPPOSING FORCES

AMERICAN

Against the Japanese defense force the Americans were to employ three Marine divisions, the 3rd, 4th and 5th, totalling over 70,000 men most of whom were seasoned veterans of earlier campaigns. Operation Detachment had already been postponed twice because of a shortage of support ships and landing craft due to the massive requirements of MacArthur's Philippines invasion, and it had to be completed in time to release men and materials for the upcoming Okinawa invasion scheduled for April 1,1945

As the plans came to fruition it was time to assemble the invasion force. The 3rd Division were still on Guam having taken the island in August, 1944, while the 4th & 5th Divisions were to be deployed from the Hawaiian Islands. The Navy was scheduled to provide a massive "softening up" bombardment prior to the invasion and many of the fleet's old battleships, the USS *Arkansas, Texas, Nevada, Idaho* and *Tennessee*, too slow for the new Task Forces that were now prowling the Pacific, were ideal for the purpose.

On February 15, the invasion fleet left Saipan, first the LSTs carrying the first waves of troops from the 4th and 5th Divisions and the following day the troop transports with the remainder of the Marines and the plethora of tanks, supplies, artillery, and supporting units. The armada was soon spotted by Japanese naval patrol aircraft and the Iwo Jima garrison went on to immediate alert. General Kuribayashi had earlier issued his troops with a document called "The Courageous Battle Vows"

Another view of the beaches with the East Boat Basin in the distance. The sign says: "Mount Suribachi 169m." (Taro Kuribayashi)

15

General Kuribayashi wasted no time in re-organizing the inadequate defense system that he discovered upon his arrival on the island. Here he is seen with members of his staff directing operations. (Taro Kuribayashi)

which stated that each man should make it his duty to kill ten of the enemy before dying. With his defenses prepared and his men ready to fight to the death, Kuribayashi waited patiently for the approaching invader.

JAPANESE

The Japanese High Command realized the importance of Iwo Jima and as early as March, 1944, began to reinforce the island. The 145th Infantry Regiment of Col Masuo Ikeda, originally intended to bolster the garrison on Saipan, was diverted to the island and in the period leading up to the Marine attack in 1945, the 109th Division, including the 2nd Mixed Brigade (MajGen Senda), 26th Tank Regiment (LtCol [Baron] Takeichi Nishi), 17th Mixed Infantry Regiment (Maj Tamachi Fujiwara), Brigade Artillery (Col Chosaku Kaido) and additional Anti-Aircraft, Mortar, Cannon and Machine Gun Battalions were drafted to the island. The Naval Units, mainly anti-aircraft, communications, supply, and engineering groups, were under the command of R/Adm Toshinosuke Ichimaru who also had charge of the 27th Air Flotilla. At the time of the Marine landing, February 19, 1945, the total Japanese garrison numbered 21,060, considerably more than the American calculation of 13,000.

OPPOSING PLANS

AMERICAN

The complexity of the underground tunnel system can be judged from this picture of one of the existing passages. (Taro Kuribayashi)

The plan of attack that was devised by MajGen Harry Schmidt's V Amphibious Corps planners looked deceptively simple. The Marines would land on the two-mile long stretch of beach between Mount Suribachi and the East Boat Basin on the south-east coast of the island. These beaches were divided into seven sections of 550yds (914m) each. Under the shadow of Suribachi lay Green Beach (1st and 2nd Bns, 28th Regt), flanked on the right by Red Beach 1 (2nd Bn, 27th Regt), Red Beach 2 (1st Bn, 27th Regt), Yellow Beach 1 (1st Bn, 23rd Regt), Yellow Beach 2 (2nd Bn, 23rd Regt), Blue Beach 1(1st and 3rd Bns, 25th Regt). Blue Beach 2 lay directly under known enemy gun emplacements in the Quarry overlooking the East Boat Basin, and it was decided that both the 1st and 3rd Bns of the 25th Regiment should land abreast on Blue Beach 1. General Cates, the 4th Division commander, said: "If I knew the name of the man on the extreme right of the right hand squad (on Blue Beach), I'd recommend him for a medal before we go in."

The 28th Regiment would attack straight across the narrowest part of the island to the opposite coast, swing left, isolate and then secure Mount Suribachi. On their right, the 27th Regiment would also cross the island and move to the north, while the 23rd Regiment would seize Airfield No. 1 and then thrust northward towards Airfield No. 2. The 25th Regiment, on the extreme right, would deploy to their right to neutralize the high ground around the Quarry overlooking the East Boat Basin.

Kuribayashi and his staff had time to pose for a formal group photograph before the Americans arrived. None was to survive the battle. (Taro Kuribayashi).

JAPANESE

General Kuribayashi's first priority was to reorganize the archaic defense system that was in place when he arrived. All civilians were sent back to the mainland as their presence could serve no useful purpose and they would be a drain on the limited supplies of food and water. With the arrival of more troops and Korean laborers he instigated a massive program of underground defenses. A complex and extensive system of tunnels, caves, gun emplacements, pillboxes, and command posts was constructed in the nine months prior to the invasion. The soft pumice-like volcanic rock was easily cut with hand tools and mixed well with cement to provide excellent reinforcement. Some tunnels were 75ft (23m) under ground, most were interconnecting, and many were provided with electric or oil lighting.

Supply points, ammunition stores, and even operating theaters were included in the system and at the height of the battle many Marines reported hearing voices and movements coming from the ground beneath them. When Mount Suribachi was isolated many of the defenders escaped to the north of the island, bypassing the Marine lines through this labyrinth of tunnels.

The tunnels were constructed at an unprecedented speed. The specification called for a minimum of 30ft (9.1m) of earth overhead to resist any shell or bomb. Most were five feet (1.5m) wide and five feet high with concrete walls and ceilings and extended in all directions (one engineer in his diary said that it was possible to walk underground for four miles). Many tunnels were built on two or even three levels and in the larger chambers, airshafts of up to 50ft (15.2m) were needed to dispel the foul air. Partially underground were the concrete blockhouses and gun

View from the south. The invasion beaches with their black sand stretch away to the right. (Taro Kuribayashi)

With Mount Suribachi in the foreground, the invasion beaches can be seen on the right of the picture, stretching northwards to the East Boat Basin. Isolating the volcano was the number one priority for the Marines and involved crossing the half-mile neck of the island as rapidly as possible. (US Navy)

sites, so well constructed that weeks of naval shelling and aerial bombing failed to damage most of them; and the hundreds of pillboxes, which were of all shapes and sizes, were usually interconnected and mutually supporting.

The General had studied earlier Japanese defense methods of attempting to halt the enemy at the beachhead and had realized that they invariably failed, and he regarded the traditional "banzai" charge as wasteful and futile. In September at Peleliu the Japanese commander, LtGen lnoue, had abandoned these outdated tactics and concentrated on attrition, wearing down the enemy from previously planned and prepared positions in the Umurbrogol Mountains. Kuribayashi approved of these tactics. He knew that the Americans would eventually take the island but he was determined to exact a fearful toll in Marine casualties before they did.

The geography of the island virtually dictated the location of the landing sites for the invasion force. From aerial photographs and periscope shots taken by the submarine USS *Spearfish*, it was obvious that there were only two stretches of beach upon which the Marines could land. General Kuribayashi had come to the same conclusion months earlier and made his plans accordingly.

Iwo Jima is some four and a half miles long with its axis running from south-west to north-east, tapering from two and a half miles wide in the north to a mere half mile in the south, giving a total land area of around seven and a half square miles. At the southern end stands Mount Suribachi, a 550ft (168m) high dormant volcano that affords commanding views over most of the island, and the beaches that stretch northward from Suribachi are the only possible sites for a landing.

On a plateau in the center of this lower part of the island the Japanese built Airfield No. 1, and further north a second plateau roughly a mile in diameter housed Airfield No. 2 and the unfinished Airfield No. 3. The

JAPANESE DEFENSE SECTORS AND US LANDING BEACHES

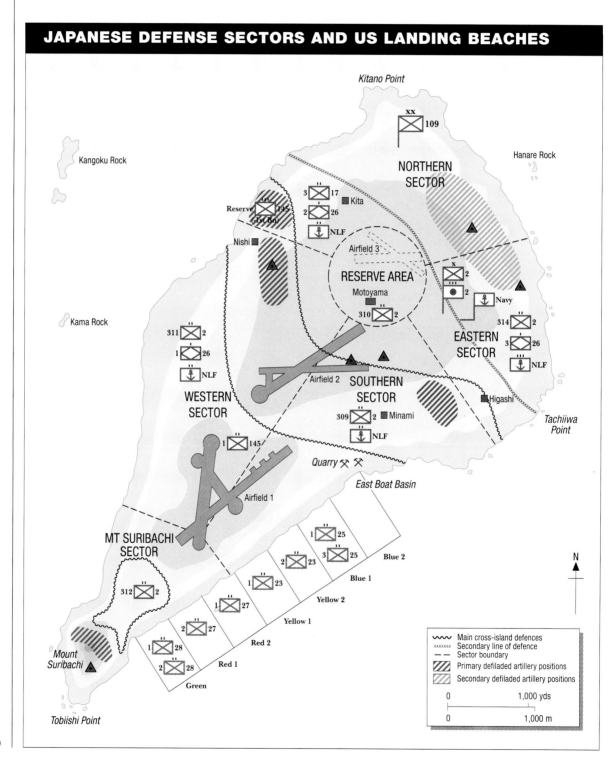

ground that slopes away from this northern plateau is a mass of valleys, ridges, gorges, and rocky outcrops that provide an ideal site for defensive fighting.

Major Yoshitaka Horie, Staff Officer to LtGen Kuribayashi, had many discussions with his superior about the role of anti-aircraft guns. Horie was of the opinion that they would be far better employed as artillery or in an anti-tank role as it was obvious that the Americans would have overwhelming air superiority before and during the battle. His reasoning seems to have impressed the General who overruled the objections of some of his staff officers and implemented some of Horie's ideas.

Horie was interviewed by a Marine officer after the war and his comments were recorded for the Marine Corps Historical Archives. He told Gen Kuribayashi: "We should change our plans so that we can use most of the anti-aircraft guns as artillery and retain very small parts of them as anti-aircraft guns. Anti-aircraft guns are good to protect the disclosed targets, especially ships, but are invaluable for the covering of land defenses," but the staff officers had different opinions. "The staff officers were inclined as follows; they said at Iwo Jima it is good to use anti-aircraft guns as both artillery and anti-aircraft guns. The natural features of Iwo are weaker than of Chichi Jima. If we have no anti-aircraft guns, our defensive positions will be completely destroyed by the enemy's air raids."

Horie continued: "And so most of the 300 anti-aircraft guns were used in both senses as above mentioned, but later, when American forces landed on Iwo Jima, those anti-aircraft guns were put to silence in one or two days and we have the evidence that most anti-aircraft guns were not valuable but 7.5cm anti-aircraft guns, prepared as anti-tank guns, were very valuable."

Horie, in his curious English, went on to describe the initial Japanese reaction to the landings: "On the February 19, American forces landed on the first airfield under cover of their keen bombardments of aircraft and warships. Although their landing direction, strength and fighting methods were same as our judgment, we could not take any counter-measures towards them, and 135 pillboxes we had at the first airfield were trodden down and occupied in only two days after their landing.

"We shot them bitterly with the artillery we had at Motoyama and Mount Suribachi, but they were immediately destroyed by the enemy's counter-firing. At that time we had opportunity to make offensive attacks against the enemy but we knew well that if we do so we will suffer many damages from American bombardments of aircraft and vessels, therefore our officers and men waited the enemy coming closer to their own positions."

THE BATTLE

D-DAY: "A NIGHTMARE IN HELL"

As a prelude to the landings MajGen Harry Schmidt, V Amphibious Corps Commander, had requested ten continuous days of shelling by battleships and cruisers of R/Adm William Blandy's Amphibious Support Force (Task Force 52). Admiral Hill rejected the request on the grounds that there would be insufficient time to re-arm his ships before D-Day. Schmidt persisted and asked for nine days. This was also turned down and he was offered a mere three days of softening up before his Marines went ashore. Spruance's comment – "I know that your people will get away with it" – was to sound hollow as the battle progressed. "Howlin' Mad" Smith was to be scathing in his criticism of the Navy's support during many of the amphibious landings throughout the Pacific campaign: "I could not forget the sight of dead Marines in the lagoon or lying on the beaches of Tarawa, men who died assaulting defenses which should have been taken out by naval gunfire," he was to write after the war.

The first day of the bombardment was a disappointment. Poor weather hampered the gunners and the results were inconclusive. Day two was to be a disaster. The cruiser USS *Pensacola* ventured too close to

Three of the old battleships of the US Navy get into position prior to "softening up" the island in preparation for the landings. Their 16in shells were ideal for reducing the concrete bunkers that dotted the Iwo Jima coastline. (National Archives)

Landing craft circle before departing for the beaches. (National Archives)

the shore and was engaged by enemy shore batteries. Six hits in rapid succession killed 17 of the crew and caused substantial damage.

Later in the day 12 gunboats (LCIs) approached to within 1,000yds (914m) of the shore as part of the support screen for over 100 "frogmen," underwater demolition teams. With distances worked out to the nearest yard from months of practice, all 12 vessels were hit by Japanese batteries and scurried away at best speed. The destroyer USS *Leutze*, which raced to their assistance, was also hit with the loss of 7 crewmen.

The final day of the bombardment was again blighted by poor weather with rainsqualls and cloud foiling the gunners. Blandy optimistically signalled Turner: "I believe that landings can be accomplished tomorrow." Schmidt complained: "We only got about 13 hours worth of fire support during the 34 hours of available daylight."

By contrast, D-Day, Monday, February 19, 1945, dawned clear and sunny with unlimited visibility. During the night Adm Marc Mitscher's Task Force 58, a vast armada of 16 carriers, 8 battleships, and 15 cruisers, fresh from highly successful attacks against the Japanese mainland, arrived off Iwo Jima accompanied by Adm Raymond Spruance in his flagship USS *Indianapolis*. Again Holland Smith was bitter, considering these raids against Japan to be an unnecessary diversion from the more important business of occupying Iwo Jima.

As the battleships and cruisers pounded the island and swarms of carrier-based aircraft mounted air strikes, the disembarkation of thousands of Marines from troopships and LVTs was gathering

A seven-knot breeze and a calm sea provided the Marines with ideal conditions for the invasion. Admiral Raymond Spruance had arrived during the night with Admiral Mitscher's mighty Task Force 58, and the island was surrounded by over 485 ships of various types to support General Schmidt's Marines. At dawn the battleships and cruisers commenced their final bombardment of Mount Suribachi and the seven invasion beaches as the Amtracs headed for the shore.

momentum. To spearhead the attack 68 LVT(A)s – armored amphibious tractors mounting a 75mm (2.95in)howitzer and three machine guns – were to venture 50yds (46m) onto the beachhead to cover the first wave of Marines, but the first of a number of planning "foul-ups" was to frustrate their deployment. Along the whole of the landing beach the Marines, LVTs, tanks, and other vehicles were to encounter 15ft high terraces of soft black volcanic ash. The troops sank up to their ankles, the vehicles to their hubcaps, and the LVTs and Sherman tanks ground to a halt within yards of the shore. The planners had described the beach conditions in glowing terms: "troops should have no difficulty in getting off the beach at any point," "the isthmus provides excellent landing beaches," and "an easy approach inland," read the pre-invasion reports.

In keeping with Gen Kuribayashi's strategy, Japanese resistance had been relatively subdued; he wanted the Americans to land substantial numbers of men onto the beaches before unleashing his well-rehearsed and co-ordinated bombardment. Many American Naval officers were under the illusion that their rolling barrage over the landing zone was responsible for the limited response.

A steady stream of small arms and machine gun fire whined across the beaches and the occasional crump of a mortar shell sent sand flying, but the most formidable enemy was the sand itself – Marines were trained to move rapidly forward; here they could only plod. The weight and amount of equipment was a terrific hindrance and various items were rapidly discarded. First to go was the gas mask, always regarded as an unnecessary trapping, and many of the Marines decided to dump their pack and retrieve it later; the most important pieces of equipment at that moment were weapons and ammunition.

As the first waves of Marines struggled to move forward, successive waves arrived at intervals of around 5 minutes and the situation rapidly deteriorated. General Kuribayashi had intended to allow the invaders to move towards Airfield No. 1 before commencing his artillery and mortar

ABOVE, LEFT **The west side of Mount Suribachi is wreathed in smoke as the pre-invasion bombardment gets under way. Spectacular as it was, Holland Smith was very disappointed with the results and criticized the Navy for years after the war for their failure to destroy most of the enemy installations before the Marines landed. (US Navy)**

barrages. The congestion on the beaches was an added bonus and a little after 1000hrs the full fury of the Japanese defenses was unleashed. From well-concealed positions ranging from the base of Mount Suribachi to the East Boat Basin a torrent of artillery, mortar, and machine gun fire rained down on the crowded beaches. Frantic messages flashed back to the control ship *Eldorado*: "troops 200yds (183m) inland pinned down," "catching all hell from the Quarry," "machine gun and artillery fire heaviest ever seen."

By 1040hrs Harry Hill had 6,000 men ashore and the bulldozers that had arrived in the early waves were hacking away at the terraces. Some tanks were breaking through to solid ground and troops were finally escaping the horror of the beaches where Kuribayashi's artillery and mortars were wreaking havoc. Robert Sherrod, a noted war correspondent for *Time-Life*, aptly described the scene as "a nightmare in hell."

At the extreme left of the beachhead, Green Beach, the terrain was less difficult where the volcanic ash gave way to rocks and stone at the base of Mount Suribachi. Here Col Harry Liversedge's 28th Regiment began their dash across the half-mile isthmus below the volcano in an attempt to isolate this strategically vital position.

On Suribachi, Col Kanehiko Atsuchi with over 2,000 men in his independent command manned a mass of artillery and mortars that were dug in around the lower slopes, and above them there were dozens of caves and tunnels all the way to the summit.

The 1st Battalion, ignoring this threat to their left flank, pressed on towards the far shore but soon encountered Capt Osada's 312th Independent Infantry Battalion and fierce fighting erupted around a series of bunkers and pillboxes. Some were destroyed and others bypassed in the mad dash to cross the island. Dead were abandoned where they lay and the wounded left in the care of the Navy Corpsmen, the heroic medical teams that accompanied all Marine operations. At 1035hrs six men of B Company, 1st Battalion reached the

ABOVE **War dogs, usually Dobermans or German Shepherds, were used extensively in the Pacific War, carrying messages and locating hidden enemy troops. They provided a very valuable service; sadly they were all destroyed at the end of the battle as it was regarded that they could not be retrained for civilian life. Here a Doberman keeps guard while his handler snatches some sleep. (National Archives)**

Abandoned landing craft on the invasion beaches. (National Archives)

General Kuribayashi had intended to let the Marines clear the beaches and head for Airfield No 1 before unleashing his well-rehearsed artillery barrage. However, as the troops became bogged down behind the terraces of volcanic ash, and with further waves of Amtracs arriving every five minutes, he seized the opportunity to rake the beaches from end to end with devastating artillery and mortar fire that caused very heavy casualties.

In a deceptively calm looking sea, rows of landing craft head for the invasion beaches, scheduled to arrive at five-minute intervals. The congestion on the beach afforded General Kuribayashi's gunners a prime target. (US Navy)

west coast, soon to be joined by the remnants of C Company and Suribachi was isolated, albeit precariously. On Red Beaches 1 and 2, the 27th Regiment under Col Thomas Wornham were having great difficulty in moving forward. The Japanese artillery bracketed the crowded beach and casualties mounted by the minute. To their right on Yellow 1 and 2, the 23rd Regiment under Col Walter Wensinger had come face to face with a mass of blockhouses and pillboxes manned by Maj Matsushita's 10th Independent Anti-Tank Battalion and Capt Awatsu's 309th Infantry Battalion. Battling against shredding machine gun fire, Sgt Darren Cole, armed only with grenades and a pistol, single-handedly silenced five pillboxes before being killed by a hand grenade and became the first of the Marine Corps 27 Medal of Honor recipients during the battle.

At the extreme right, Blue Beach 1, Col John Lanigan's 25th Regiment moved straight ahead to avoid the obvious danger presented by the high ground at the Quarry on their right flank, making a two-pronged attack with the 1st Battalion pressing inland as the 3rd Battalion swung right to assault cliffs at the base of the Quarry.

2nd Lt Benjamin Roselle, part of a six-man naval gunfire team, was to suffer a horrendous D-Day. Reaching the second row of terraces, they were pinned down by heavy artillery fire. As they attempted to move forward, the radio operator went down and Roselle strapped his equipment to his back and moved on. Within a minute a mortar shell exploded among the group. Others were able to move but the Lieutenant could not, his left foot and ankle hung from his leg, held on by a ribbon of flesh. Pinned down and with no hope of advancing, he rode out the storm of mortar shells that were blasting the area. Within

minutes a second round landed near him and fragments tore into his other leg. For nearly an hour he wondered where the next shell would land. He was soon to find out as a shell burst almost on top of him, wounding him for the third time in the shoulder. Almost at once another explosion bounced him several feet into the air and hot shards ripped into both thighs. Remarkably, he wondered what time it was and as he lifted his arm to look at his watch a mortar shell exploded only feet away and blasted the watch from his wrist and tore a large jagged hole in his forearm: "I was beginning to know what it must be like to be crucified," he was to say later. Eventually recovered by a medical team, he was taken to an offshore LST hospital ship where his fractured arm was set and his foot amputated.

A few tanks of the 4th Tank Battalion had succeeded in getting ashore on Blue 1 at around 1020hrs. A tank-dozer scooped a passage through the first terrace and the remainder passed through in single file, only halting when they reached a large minefield.

At 1400hrs the 3rd Battalion under their commander "Jumpin' Joe" Chambers began scaling the cliffs around the Quarry. The enemy resistance was fanatical and the Marines were soon down to 150 men from the original 900 who had landed at 0900hrs.

At the base of Mount Suribachi the 28th Regiment were consolidating their positions. LT Keith Wells' 3rd Platoon were ordered to cross the isthmus to reinforce the 1st Platoon whose position was in danger of being overrun. Under heavy fire from their left the four squads sprinted forward, coming across many dead and wounded Marines who had to be left behind until the base of the volcano had been secured. By afternoon a few Sherman tanks that had penetrated the beachhead were moving up to provide valuable assistance by destroying many Japanese pillboxes with their 75mm (2.95in) guns, and by evening Suribachi was securely isolated from the rest of the island.

The grim task of occupying this formidable bastion would have to wait until later.

In the center, the 27th and 25th Regiments were gradually extricating themselves from the Red and Yellow beaches and moving towards Airfield No. 1. The Seabees (Naval Construction Battalions), largely recruited from the civilian construction industry and manned by volunteers usually in their 40s or early 50s, were performing miracles on the beaches. Landing with the early waves of assault troops they attacked the terraces with their bulldozers carving passages through which the tanks, artillery, and transport could pass and cleared the masses of bogged down landing craft and vehicles that cluttered the shoreline. There was a joke: "Protect your Seabees. One of them could be your dad." Turner had had to halt the landings around 1300hrs as there was nowhere to get more Marines ashore, but the heroic efforts of the Seabees, who suffered heavy casualties on D-Day, allowed the flow of men and materials to resume after two hours. Even so, in virtually every shell hole there lay at least one dead Marine and at the foot of the terraces scores of wounded lay among the exploding shells and mortars, waiting for evacuation by the landing craft which were running the gauntlet of the terrific barrage.

By 1130hrs some Marines had reached the southern end of Airfield No. 1 which was sited on a plateau whose perimeter rose steeply on the eastern side. The Japanese mounted a fierce defense, hundreds being killed and the remainder pouring across the runway or disappearing into the pipes of the drainage system. At one point over a hundred Japanese charged down the runway to be met by a hail of machine gun and rifle fire.

As evening approached, the Marines held a line running from the base of Mount Suribachi across the southern perimeter of Airfield No. 1 and ending at the foot of the Quarry, (See Map). The 0-1 line, the D-Day

On the beach a Marine in pensive mood sits with his M1 rifle. (National Archives)

objective, had not been reached but it was always an unrealistic goal. Perhaps if Adm Nimitz had prised some of his deskbound planners away from their comfortable offices in Hawaii and given them a spell with the assault troops they may have come up with more realistic projections.

The Marines habitually sought to consolidate their positions during the night while the Japanese, on the other hand, were adept at nighttime infiltration and favored darkness for their famous "banzai" charges. Throughout the night destroyers fired flares to illuminate the front lines. As they descended on parachutes they cast an eerie glow over the scene. The Japanese kept up their mortar and artillery fire, while at sea a shuttle service of landing craft brought in supplies and evacuated the wounded.

Aboard the command ship *Eldorado*, "Howlin' Mad" Smith studied the day's reports. Progress had not been as good as he had hoped and the casualty figures made grim reading: "I don't know who he is, but the Japanese General running this show is one smart bastard," he announced to a group of war correspondents.

D+1 – D+5: "INFLICT MUCH DAMAGE TO THE ENEMY"

D+1

A four-foot high surf on the beaches and a bitterly cold wind did little to raise the spirits of either the Marines or their commanders on Tuesday, D+1. Having isolated Mount Suribachi, the 28th Regiment were faced with the unenviable task of capturing it, while to the north the remainder of the invasion force were poised to mount a concerted attack to secure Airfields 1 and 2.

With daylight came the carrier planes, pounding the volcano with bombs and napalm while destroyers shelled the gun positions directly to

Section Chief Marine Private First Class R. F. Callahan calls in 155mm (6.1in) artillery fire against a Japanese position. (USMC)

the front of the 28th Regiment. Attacking on a broad front with artillery support, the Marines could only gain 75yds (69m) of ground by 1200hrs in the face of fierce resistance from Col Atsuchi's defenders. Tanks had joined the battle at around 1100hrs following long delays in refuelling and added valuable support, but the Japanese had a huge advantage in their prepared positions on the higher ground. Looking ahead, Lt Wells said: "I saw little or nothing to shield us from the enemy's fire power; my men would be open targets all the way."

Colonel Atsuchi radioed Gen Kuribayashi that the American bombardments from both artillery and offshore naval units were very fierce and suggested that he and his men should attempt a "banzai" charge. The General had expected the garrison on Mount Suribachi to maintain control for at least ten days and did not even bother to reply, but suspected that Atsuchi was beginning to waver.

Little progress was made in the afternoon and the Marines dug in and awaited reinforcements and additional tanks for an all-out assault the following day. The Japanese were determined that there should be no respite for the enemy and commenced a barrage all along the front line. "The shells continued walking up our lines, exploding only a few feet away. All I could think about was the great loss of men. What made it even more horrifying, it stopped soon after passing through us and started back again," said Wells. During the night, Japanese troops began to gather near the eastern slopes of the volcano but the destroyer USS *Henry A. Wiley* blasted them under the glare of searchlights, and the anticipated nighttime counterattack was nipped in the bud.

To the north, the other three regiments began their offensive at around 0830hrs, with the right flank anchored at the Quarry and the left swinging north in an attempt to straighten the line. The Marines encountered strong opposition from the mass of bunkers, pillboxes, and landmines that had been so carefully prepared. Mid-afternoon saw the arrival of the brand new battleship USS *Washington* which blasted the cliffs around the Quarry with its massive 16in guns causing a landslide that blocked dozens of enemy caves.

By 1200hrs the majority of Airfield No. 1 was in American hands, a bitter blow to Gen Kuribayashi who had not anticipated such a rapid advance, and the Marines now had an almost straight front line across the island although the D-Day 0-1 objective still eluded them. General Schmidt decided to commit the 21st Regiment of the 3rd Division, an indication that the top brass did not consider that progress had been swift enough. (The Joint Chiefs of Staff had hoped to keep the whole of the 3rd Division intact for the upcoming invasion of Okinawa.) However, the high seas and congested beaches frustrated the landings and after six hours in their landing craft the Regiment were ordered back to their transports.

As the second day drew to a close the Marines had control of almost a quarter of the island but the cost had been very heavy. Kuribayashi's orders, "Each man should think of his defense position as his graveyard, fight until the last and inflict much damage to the enemy" was bearing fruit. Heavy rain began to fall in the afternoon and continued throughout the night, filling foxholes with water and collapsing their sides. The old hands among the Marines shivered and wished themselves back among the hot sands of the atolls that they had so recently liberated.

D+2

Wednesday's plan looked straightforward – the 28th Regiment would begin their final assault on Mount Suribachi and the remainder would

The beaches were already beginning to become congested with swamped jeeps, trucks, and tanks as this group of Marines await their chance to move out. (National Archives)

A machine gun crew sit among a pile of spent ammunition somewhere just south of Mount Suribachi. (National Archives)

move north on a broad front: in the west, the 26th and 27th Regiments, in the center the 23rd and in the east the 24th, but simple plans seldom develop smoothly. The bad weather of the previous day had deteriorated even further as a howling gale tore through the island and rain clouds scurried overhead. Six-foot waves crashed down onto the beaches forcing Adm Turner to close them down again.

For an 18 year old Marine in his first battle, Iwo Jima was a trying experience for "Chuck" Tatum, a member of a machine gun squad with the 27th Regiment: "Dawn on D+2 greeted us with a cold rain and we were still next to Airfield No. 1. I worked this out to be a grand total of 1,000yds (914m) advance from the beach in two days – we wouldn't be arrested for speeding! The terrain we were in was flat from the edge of the runway to the western shoreline, probably the only flat ground in Iwo. The dark overcast sky filled with rain, soaked us, and transformed the volcanic soil into a gooey sticky mess. Vehicles and men struggled to move and finally bogged down. On the landing beaches to our right chaos continued as increasing winds and seas smashed derelict, broached landing craft. Beaches remained closed to all but emergency traffic and wounded lay patiently in hastily prepared shelters while Corpsmen did what they could to save lives. At 0800hrs the frontal attack northward was renewed. The 5th Division objective was the left flank of the island, the entire area between the runways and the beaches. As we had the day before, we mopped up bypassed positions and consolidated the gains made."

Supported by a blistering artillery barrage, fire from Navy cruisers and destroyers, and napalm and machine gun fire from over 40 carrier planes, the 28th Regiment launched their assault on Mount Suribachi at

0845hrs. The gunfire denuded the ground before them, revealing chains of blockhouses and connecting trenches with little or no cover between the two front lines. There was the additional hazard of rows of barbed wire that the Marines had placed in front of their own lines during the night to prevent enemy infiltration. It had been assumed that the morning's advance would be spearheaded by tanks which would flatten all before them but again they were delayed by fuelling problems.

The 3rd Platoon in the center met heavy opposition but the late arrival of tanks and halftrack 75mm (2.95in) guns helped their progress. By evening the regiment had formed a semi-circle around the north side of the volcano and moved forward 650yds (594m) on the left, 500yds (457m) in the center and 1,000yds (914m) on the right, – good progress under the circumstances.

"We had nothing to protect us but the clothes on our back," said Wells who was in the thick of the fighting, reducing enemy bunkers with hand grenades and receiving severe wounds to his legs. "I could feel myself running out of energy, my wounds were beginning to take their toll. I had not eaten, drunk water, or defecated in two and a half days."

To the north, 68 Navy planes blasted the Japanese lines with bombs and rockets, and at 0740hrs a massive barrage of artillery and naval gunfire added their weight as the 4th and 5th Marine Divisions moved against a complex of well-hidden enemy positions and casualties soon began to mount. Near the west coast, Sherman tanks led an advance of over 1,000 yards by the 26th and 27th Regiments and the D-Day 0-1 line was finally reached. On the east side of the island, the 4th Division could only take 50yds (46m) of ground in the rugged terrain around the Quarry despite being reinforced by an extra company. Fighting among the cliffs and caves in the Quarry area was a hazardous business and involved heavy casualties. Capt "Jumpin' Joe" McCarthy, commanding officer of G Company 2nd Battalion of the 24th Regiment states: "We

With Mount Suribachi just visible at the left, these troops have moved off the beaches and are heading inland. Rows of pillboxes and minefields were to bar their way to the airfield. (US Navy)

Navy Pharmacist's Mate First Class Jack Ente, attached to the 3rd Marine Division huddles in a blanket on Iwo Jima. Veterans of South Pacific battles were unaccustomed to the cooler climates of the Volcano Islands. (USMC)

landed with 257 men and received 90 replacements. Of that total of 347 only 35 men were able to walk off the island when the fighting was over." McCarthy's men were under terrific fire all morning and were suffering heavy losses and in the afternoon he assigned an assault squad to clean out the pillboxes that had kept his advance to a standstill.

One of the group was Pfc Pete Santoro who recalls: "I took it on myself to go to my left as the others moved right, and below me was the entrance to a tunnel. I saw two Japs with rifles crawling out on their hands and knees. I shot them both in the back I'm sorry to say as I don't know how to say turn around in Japanese. Captain McCarthy came around the other side and shot them again and I said I got them already. As we went to take more high ground I found the entrance to another tunnel. I fired a rifle grenade but it fell short so I fired my last one. As I started to move in I was shot in the back. It felt like I was hit with a sledgehammer. I couldn't move my legs. I crawled out to two of our men who asked if I had been hit by a shotgun. The Jap had hit my M1 ammunition clip and my shells had shattered and penetrated all over my back." Santoro was eventually taken to the hospital ship *Solace* and after treatment returned to the beach.

It was here that he disposed of a Japanese sniper who had been taking potshots at airmen from Airfield No. 1, and from there he returned to his unit much to the surprise of McCarthy who put him in charge of the ammunition dump. On March 9, a mortar round exploded close by and Santoro was severely concussed. Returning again to the *Solace*, he swore that he would not be returning to that island.

General Schmidt again disembarked the 21st Regiment of the 3rd Division and they came ashore on Yellow Beach. The Japanese continued their disruptive fire throughout the night and between 150 and 200 troops gathered at the end of the runway of Airfield No. 2 and rushed the lines of the 23rd Regiment at 2330hrs. A combination of artillery and naval gunfire annihilated them before they could reach the Marines.

The ships of the Navy Task Force supporting the landings were to become the targets of one of the early kamikaze attacks of the war. As the light began to fade, 50 Japanese aircraft approached from the north-west. They were from the 2nd Milate Special Attack Unit based at Katori Airbase and had refuelled at Hachijo Jima 125 miles south of Tokyo. They were picked up by the radar of the USS *Saratoga*, a veteran carrier of the Pacific War, and six fighters were sent to intercept. They shot down two Zeros (Mitsubishi AGM fighters), but the remaining Zeros plowed on through the low lying cloud, two of them trailing smoke, and slammed into the side of the carrier turning the hangers into an inferno. Another solitary attacker smashed into the flight deck leaving a gaping hole 100yds (91m) from the bow. Damage control teams worked wonders and within one hour the fires were under control and the Saratoga was able to recover a few of her planes. The others were taken aboard the escort carriers USS *Wake Island* and USS *Natoma Bay*.

Another aircraft, a "Betty" twin engined bomber (Mitsubishi G4M), tore into the escort carrier USS *Bismarck Sea*. The decks were full of aircraft and the ensuing explosion caused uncontrollable fires. Abandon ship was sounded and 800 men went over the side. Within a few minutes a huge explosion ripped off the entire stern of the carrier and she rolled over and sank. Three other ships were also damaged: the escort carrier

Near the base of Mount Suribachi, Marines destroy an enemy position with demolition charges. The dash across the base of Suribachi was accomplished in good time, the capture of the volcano taking days longer. (USMC)

USS *Lurga Point* was showered with flaming debris as four aircraft were blasted out of the sky; the minesweeper *Keokuk* was damaged when a "Jill" dive bomber (Nakajima B6N) hit her deck; and LST 477 loaded with Sherman tanks received a glancing blow.

The *Saratoga*, with destroyer escort, returned to Pearl Harbor, but by the time the damage was repaired the war was over. The kamikazes had done their work well: 358 men killed, one carrier sunk, and another severely damaged. It was a grim preview of the mayhem they would later cause during the invasion of Okinawa in April.

D+3

There was no let-up in the weather on Wednesday as Marines of the 28th Regiment, drenched to the skin and bent by the wind, prepared to renew the attack on Suribachi. Fresh supplies of ammunition had been brought to the front during the night, but the Shermans were mired in mud and the Navy declined to supply air support in the appalling weather. It was to be up to the foot soldier with rifle, flamethrower, grenade, and demolition charge to win the day.

Colonel Atsuchi still had 800–900 men left and they had no intention of allowing the Americans an easy victory. Major Youamata announced: "We are surrounded by enemy craft of all sizes, shapes and descriptions, enemy shells have smashed at our installations and defenses, their planes bomb and strafe yet we remain strong and defiant. The Americans are beginning to climb the first terraces towards our defenses. Now they shall taste our steel and lead."

Throughout the day the Marines attacked the Japanese positions on the lower slopes of Mount Suribachi. There was little room for maneuver and it was impossible to use support fire from artillery and tanks to maximum advantage because of the close proximity of the lines. By

afternoon, patrols from Companies G and E had worked their way around the base of the volcano and it was surrounded. The bitter fighting on the northern slopes had reduced the Japanese garrison to a few hundred men and many were infiltrating the Marine lines through the maze of tunnels and joining Kuribayashi's forces in the north. Others moved upwards towards the summit. The final assault would have to wait until the following day.

The sweep to the north continued with Harry Schmidt placing the newly landed 3rd Division reinforcements, the 21st Regiment, in the center of the line between the 4th and 5th Divisions around Airfield No. 2. Here Col Ikeda with his 145th Regiment had the strongest section of the Japanese defenses. Lack of sleep and hot food, heavy casualties, and terrible weather were affecting the fighting efficiency of the men who had landed on D-Day and many of the hard pressed units were replaced. The new 3rd Division men had a baptism of fire as they stormed the heavily defended ground south of the airfield and the day's gains amounted to a mere 250yds (229m) – F Company of the 2nd Battalion were so badly mauled that they only lasted one day.

On the eastern flank near the Quarry, "Jumpin' Joe" Chambers had rocket firing trucks brought forward to pound the enemy hideouts, resulting in dozens of Japanese fleeing to the lower ground where they were decimated by machine gun fire. Chambers was himself badly wounded in the afternoon and evacuated to a hospital ship.

The Japanese mounted a series of strong counterattacks throughout the day which were repulsed by heavy artillery fire, and as the weather

The Sherman tanks had great difficulty coming ashore until the bulldozers could clear a way for them through the soft sand. Here. "Cairo," fitted with wooden planks as protection against magnetic mines, has shed a track. (National Archives)

deteriorated further with icy rain and low mists preventing the Navy from providing gunfire and air support, the fighting died down. Casualties still crowded the beaches as the rough seas prevented LSTs from evacuating the wounded, and behind the lines near Airfield No. 1, the 4th Division cemetery was inaugurated. Up till now the dead had been left in rows under their ponchos, "stacked like cordwood" as one Marine described it.

"Howlin' Mad" Smith aboard the USS *Auburn* was counting the cost. Three days of battle and the Regimental Returns listed 2,517 casualties for the 4th Division and 2,057 for the 5th: 4,574 dead and wounded and the 0-1 line had just been reached. Little did he know that as his Marines approached the hills, ravines, canyons, gullies, and cliffs of the north the worst was yet to come.

D+4

February 23 was the day that the 28th Regiment captured Mount Suribachi. General Kuribayashi had not expected this strategically important feature to fall so early in the battle and when the survivors who had infiltrated the American lines arrived in the north they were severely reprimanded.

With much improved weather, LtCol Chandler Johnson gave the order to occupy and secure the summit and Marines from the 3rd Platoon started out at 0800hrs. A forty-man patrol led by Lt Hal

ABOVE **Near the beach, rows of dead lie under their ponchos: burial parties check identification and personal possessions. (National Archives)**

RIGHT **Marine artillery was vital in the support of the front line troops. Most of the Marine advances were accompanied by massive bombardments from both offshore naval units and forward artillery. (National Archives)**

Schrier labored up the northern slopes, laden with weapons and ammunition. The going became increasingly difficult but the opposition was surprisingly light. At 1000hrs they reached the rim of the crater and engaged a number of the enemy who attacked them with hand grenades. At 1020hrs the Stars and Stripes were raised on a length of pipe and *Leatherneck* photographer Lou Lowery recorded the moment. Throughout the southern half of the island the shout was "the flag is up" and troops cheered and vessels sounded their sirens. Around 1200hrs, a larger flag was raised to replace the smaller one and the event was photographed by Associated Press cameraman Joe Rosenthal, and this became the most famous picture of World War II. (For a full account of the flag raisings on Mount Suribachi see Appendix 3.)

With about one third of Iwo Jima in American hands and a great improvement in the weather, Gen Harry Schmidt and Gen Cates came ashore to set up their HQs (Gen Rockey had come ashore the previous day), and the three met to discuss the situation. It was decided that the 3rd Division would maintain the center with the 5th Division in the west and the 4th in the east. The Navy would continue to add support with gunfire and carrier aircraft, and the tanks of all three divisions would come under a single command, LtCol William Collins of the 5th Division.

D+4 was largely a day of consolidation and replenishment although fighting continued south of Airfield No. 2 and north of the Quarry. Schmidt was planning a major offensive for the following day in an attempt to break the stalemate.

D+5

True to his word, Harry Schmidt provided a tremendous barrage all along the front line. From the west the battleship USS *Idaho* blasted the

Flamethrowers were invaluable on Iwo Jima where the enemy had to be prised out of every cave, pillbox, and bunker by groups of Marines. A flamethrower was always accompanied by a number of riflemen to protect him against snipers. (US Navy)

Colonel Kenehiko Atsuchi had established a formidable defense sector on Mount Suribachi. At the base a network of cave defenses, mortar, artillery and machine-gun positions thwarted the advance of the 28th Marines for four days, while further up the volcano, numerous emplacements were to hamper the Marines right up to February 23rd, when the flag was raised on the summit.

By D+1, the 28th Marines had established a secure line across the island and were supported by heavy 103mm (4.1in) artillery fire from the 13th Marines to their rear. General Kuribayashi knew that severing Mount Suribachi from the northern plateau had done little to damage his overall defense system, and had decided that the volcano should be a semi-independent sector capable of continuing the battle without his assistance.

The only route to the top of Mount Suribachi lay up the north face in the 2nd Battalion's zone. At 0900hrs on D+4, Col Johnson sent out two patrols from Companies D and F to reconnoiter suitable routes and little resistance was forthcoming. A 40-man detachment followed them and the rim of the volcano was reached at about 1015hrs, where a short fierce skirmish developed with the few remaining defenders, who were soon overwhelmed.

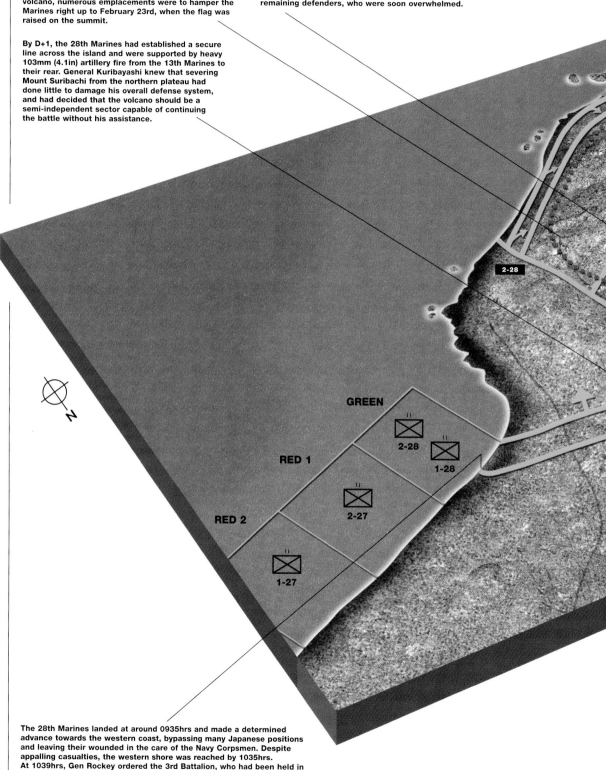

The 28th Marines landed at around 0935hrs and made a determined advance towards the western coast, bypassing many Japanese positions and leaving their wounded in the care of the Navy Corpsmen. Despite appalling casualties, the western shore was reached by 1035hrs.
At 1039hrs, Gen Rockey ordered the 3rd Battalion, who had been held in reserve, to land in support of the 1st and 2nd.

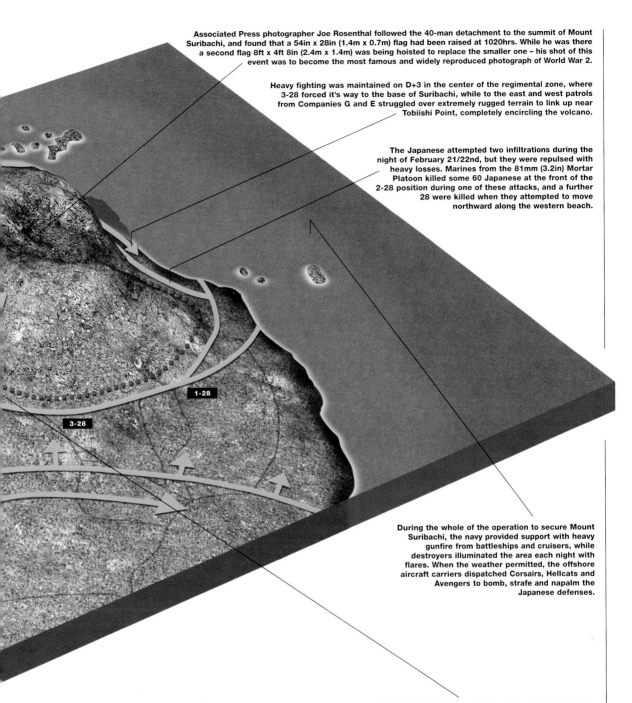

Associated Press photographer Joe Rosenthal followed the 40-man detachment to the summit of Mount Suribachi, and found that a 54in x 28in (1.4m x 0.7m) flag had been raised at 1020hrs. While he was there a second flag 8ft x 4ft 8in (2.4m x 1.4m) was being hoisted to replace the smaller one – his shot of this event was to become the most famous and widely reproduced photograph of World War 2.

Heavy fighting was maintained on D+3 in the center of the regimental zone, where 3-28 forced it's way to the base of Suribachi, while to the east and west patrols from Companies G and E struggled over extremely rugged terrain to link up near Tobiishi Point, completely encircling the volcano.

The Japanese attempted two infiltrations during the night of February 21/22nd, but they were repulsed with heavy losses. Marines from the 81mm (3.2in) Mortar Platoon killed some 60 Japanese at the front of the 2-28 position during one of these attacks, and a further 28 were killed when they attempted to move northward along the western beach.

1-28

3-28

During the whole of the operation to secure Mount Suribachi, the navy provided support with heavy gunfire from battleships and cruisers, while destroyers illuminated the area each night with flares. When the weather permitted, the offshore aircraft carriers dispatched Corsairs, Hellcats and Avengers to bomb, strafe and napalm the Japanese defenses.

D+2 saw the Marines surrounding the base of Mount Suribachi from coast to coast. In the west were 1st Battalion, in the center the 3rd Battalion, and in the east the 2nd Battalion. Tanks did not participate in the early phases of this assault because they were unable to refuel and rearm in time as their maintenance section had not yet come ashore.

ASSAULT ON MOUNT SURIBACHI D-DAY - D+4

The 28th Marines landed on Green Beach and advanced across the 700yds (640m) wide isthmus at the base of Mount Suribachi. Despite fierce opposition and very heavy casualties, they had isolated the volcano and its defenders by 1035hrs. General Kuribayashi had anticipated that Suribachi would be cut off early in the battle, but was very disappointed that Col Atsuchi's garrison held out for only four days.

An armored Amtrac, "Old Glory" somewhere on the island. (National Archives)

area north of the airfield with her 14in guns as the cruiser USS *Pensacola*, repaired after her D-Day battering, joined in from the east coast. Masses of aircraft added bombs and rockets, and the Marine artillery and mortars expended huge amounts of ammunition.

The attack was spearheaded by the 21st Regiment deployed in the area between the two airfields. Massed tanks were scheduled to precede the infantry but Col Ikeda had anticipated this move, and the taxiways of both airfields were heavily mined and covered by anti-tank guns. The first two tanks were disabled by mines and the remainder ground to a halt. Deprived of their armor, the Marines had no alternative but to clear the mass of bunkers and pillboxes the hard way, with small arms, grenades and flamethrowers. In what looked more like an episode from World War I, the Marines charged the high ground and the Japanese retaliated by leaving their positions and engaging the Americans in hand-to-hand fighting. In a frenzied mêlée of clubbing, stabbing, kicking and punching, arms and legs were broken, swords slashed, bodies fell and blood spurted until over fifty of the enemy lay dead and the Marines occupied the higher ground.

With only four hours of daylight remaining, the Marines, exhausted and desperately short of ammunition, were determined to hold on to their gains. As the light faded the redoubtable Seabees came forward with tractors and trailers loaded with ammunition, food, and water and the troops settled in for the night. Warrant Office George Green remembers the incident well: "The Seabees had loaded trailers with supplies and ammunition and brought them to the limit of Airfield No. 1, only 200yds (183m) from the battlefront. As darkness fell the entrenched Marines stared in wonder as a tractor trundled towards them towing a trailer with ammunition, water, and containers of hot food preceded by two men on foot carrying flashlights to show the way. How they did it I don't know. After dark we heard the tractor coming, and sure enough there's a guy driving the thing in pitch-black night. To this day I don't know how he knew where he was going. To me that guy had guts."

On the right flank, the 24th Regiment of the 4th Division were battling for "Charlie Dog Ridge," an escarpment south of the main runway of Airfield No. 2. Backed up by howitzers and mortars they blasted and burned their way to the top sustaining heavy casualties. At 1700hrs Col Walter Jordan ordered the men to dig in for the night. By Iwo Jima standards the overall gains for the day had been impressive, but so too had the casualty figures. Between D+1 and D+5, 1,034 men had died, 3,741 were wounded, 5 were missing and 558 were suffering from battle fatigue. Less than half of the island had been secured and the battle had a further 30 days to run.

D+6 – D+11: INTO THE MEATGRINDER

D+6

Having secured a front across the island that approximated to the 0-1 line, Harry Schmidt was intent on pressing northward across the plateau and the unfinished Airfield No. 3 to the north coast to split the enemy in two. Other factors also influenced the commander's choice. The west coast of the island had accessible beaches which were desperately needed to unload the vast amount of equipment and

The opening up of the beaches on the west side of the island was vital. Little could be landed on the east coast until the masses of vehicles and equipment was cleared. (National Archives)

supplies still stacked in the armada of transports. With Okinawa only two months away these ships were urgently needed elsewhere, but at the moment the Japanese still commanded the heights north-west of Airfield No. 2 from which they could shell the western coast with impunity.

Even though the southern end of the island was still within range of many of the Japanese guns, the area around Airfield No. 1 was being turned into a gigantic construction site. Over 2,000 Seabees were extending the runways to make them capable of handling the giant B29 Superfortress bombers, P51 Mustang fighters, and P61 Black Widow night fighters. Off the shores of Mount Suribachi, a base was being established for the Catalina and Coronado flying boats engaged in rescue operations between the Marianas and Japan. Elsewhere a "city" of Nissan huts, tents, workshops, and supply dumps was replacing what only days earlier had been a bloody battlefield.

The thrust to the north began on D+6, Sunday, February 25 – no day of rest for the Marines. As the 3rd Battalion moved against high ground at the end of the main runway of Airfield No. 2, 26 Shermans rumbled out to spearhead the attack and ran into a fusillade of artillery, anti-tank gun, and mortar fire. Three of the leading tanks burst into flames and were abandoned. The strongest point in the Japanese defenses was "Hill Peter," a 360ft high prominence just off the runway. This was stormed repeatedly but by 1430hrs the Marines had only gained 200yds (183m). The 2nd and 1st Battalions had slightly better luck and were north of the airfield, although "Hill Peter" remained in enemy hands. Nine Shermans had been knocked out and Marine casualties stood at nearly 400 dead and wounded.

The 5th Division on the left were already 400yds (366m) ahead of the 3rd Division lines and were ordered to stay where they were, but on the right the 4th Division faced a complex of four formidable defense positions that became known collectively as the "Meatgrinder." The first was Hill 382 (named from its elevation above sea level), with its slopes peppered with countless pillboxes and caves. Four hundred yards to the south lay a shallow depression called the "Amphitheater," and immediately to the east

Rocket firing trucks were used extensively on Iwo Jima where the terrain permitted. It was usual for the trucks to line up, fire off their rockets as fast as possible, and get the hell out before the Japanese mortars located them. (National Archives)

The most famous photograph of World War II. Associated Press cameraman Joe Rosenthal's superb shot of Marines raising the flag on the summit of Mount Suribachi on February 23, 1945. (US Navy)

was "Turkey Knob," a hill surmounted by a massive blockhouse. The fourth obstacle was the ruins of the village of Minami, long reduced to rubble by naval gunfire and now studded with machine gun emplacements. This collective killing ground was defended by MajGen Senda and his 2nd Mixed Brigade which included the men of Baron Nishi's 26th Tank Regiment, now largely devoid of tanks but still full of fight.

The 23rd and 24th Regiments, some 3,800 men of the 4th Division, little knowing that this was the island's most impregnable fortress, prepared to take on the "Meatgrinder" and at 0800hrs the now customary naval barrage and armada of carrier planes preceded the assault on Hill 382. One platoon battled their way to the summit only to be surrounded when the Japanese mounted a massive counterattack. Vicious hand to hand fighting ensued as the survivors withdrew under cover of smoke. Ten of the wounded were recovered after dark by gallant volunteers, and day one in the "Meatgrinder" was a complete stalemate. About 100yds (91m) had been gained at the cost of nearly 500 casualties.

D+7

Monday, February 26, dawned bright but chilly. The Marines could not believe that they had only been on the island for a week; it seemed like months. "Hill Peter" remained defiant and at 0800hrs the 9th Regiment advanced with tank support. One flamethrower tank got behind the enemy lines and incinerated a number of the enemy who were escaping through a tunnel, but the day's gains were insignificant.

To the west the 5th Division set their sights on Hill 362A, 600yds (549m) south of the village of Nishi and surrounded by pillboxes and

49

Bogged down tank, Amtracs blown over by shellfire – a view on the beaches taken some days after the landing. (National Archives)

caves. Tanks from the 5th Tank Battalion ground through the rocks and boulders to give support but the complex proved impregnable. A little to the right, the tanks smashed through the enemy defenses to a depth of 100yds (91m), and the 27th Regiment advanced up the west coast assisted by gunfire from the Amphibious Battalions from offshore. Day two of the battle for Hill 382 in the "Meatgrinder" saw the 24th Regiment replaced by the 25th Regiment. The initial attack looked promising with a gain of over 100yds (91m) until heavy machine gun fire from "Turkey Knob" brought the advance to a halt.

The 23rd Regiment to the left worked its way through a minefield beside the perimeter track of the airfield and advanced towards a ruined radio station at the foot of the hill. A massive fusillade of mortar and machine gun fire from nearby "Turkey Knob" and Hill 382 brought the Marines to a grinding halt as 17 men lay dead and 26 were wounded. Under cover of smoke grenades, stretcher-bearers evacuated the survivors. It was during this engagement that Pvt Douglas Jacobson silenced sixteen enemy positions using a bazooka single-handedly. The 19-year-old had killed 75 of the enemy in less than 30 minutes and earned himself the Medal of Honor.

D+8

"Hill Peter" still stood out like a sore thumb at the front of the 3rd Division line and at 0800hrs two battalions of the 9th regiment, LtCol Randall's 1st and LtCol Cushman's 2nd, moved forward to secure the complex. Inching forward against murderous machine gun and

As tanks assembled near Airfield No. 2, Marines of G Company 24th Regiment relax before renewing the attack on enemy pillboxes in the area. (USMC)

mortar fire the 1st reached the top of the hill but were pinned down by fire from bypassed positions at their rear. In the early afternoon another concerted effort was launched and elements of both battalions relieved the beleaguered Marines.

To the east the 4th Division appeared to be bogged down before the seemingly impregnable "Meatgrinder." General Cates committed five battalions to the area, two against Hill 382 and three against "Turkey Knob," and all day the battle seesawed up and down the slopes of the hill. Rocket launching trucks blasted the hill with over 500 rockets before having to scurry away under a torrent of enemy mortar fire, and at one point a small group of Marines actually reached the summit until shortage of ammunition and vicious counterattacks forced them to fall back. At the foot of the hill the Marines finally completed an encircling maneuver after bitter hand-to-hand fighting, and the last hours of daylight were spent in consolidating their precarious gains.

As the battle moved further north the tanks found it more and more difficult to operate among the gullies and boulder-strewn terrain. Tankdozers, Shermans fitted with bulldozer blades, were constantly in action clearing paths through the rubble and scrubland but the battle was developing into a horrific man-to-man slog in which casualties escalated by the day and prisoners were a novelty. The only grim consolation for the Marines was that their casualties could be replaced.

During the night, Japanese aircraft made a desperate attempt to get supplies to their garrison. In the only attempt that was made during the battle to support their troops, the aircraft succeeded in dropping a few parachutes containing medical supplies and ammunition. Three of the planes were shot down by carrier based night fighters. General Kuribayashi was moved to say: "I pay many respects to these brave aviators. It is difficult to express how the fighting youth of Iwo Jima who stood before their death felt when they saw these brave flyers."

Hill 382 was surrounded by minefields and it fell to the infantryman to assault the Hill with flamethrowers, satchel charges and grenades. One Platoon reached the summit only to be surrounded when the Japanese mounted a counter-attack, and the survivors had to be evacuated under cover of smoke. Day one in the Meatgrinder was a complete stalemate – 100yds (91m) gained at the cost of nearly 500 casualties.

The 23rd and 24th Marines of the 4th Division, some 3800 men, began their assault on the Meatgrinder at 0800hrs on D+6. The customary naval barrage and sorties by carrier based bombers and fighters preceded the Marines, and Sherman tanks spearheaded the attack, but the terrain proved to be so rough that they had to divert through the 3rd Division lines and progress from the left flank: an ominous sign of the growing limitations of tank support in the appalling conditions.

By D+12, the heaviest opposition was concentrated on high ground north-east of the bypassed Hill 382, the Minami area, and in the south, where the Amphitheater and Turkey Knob were still in enemy hands, despite six days of continuous bombardment. Shermans of the 4th Tank Battalion led the day's assault, in which units of the 23rd Marines neared the blockhouse on top of Turkey Knob, but were repulsed by machine-gun and small arms fire.

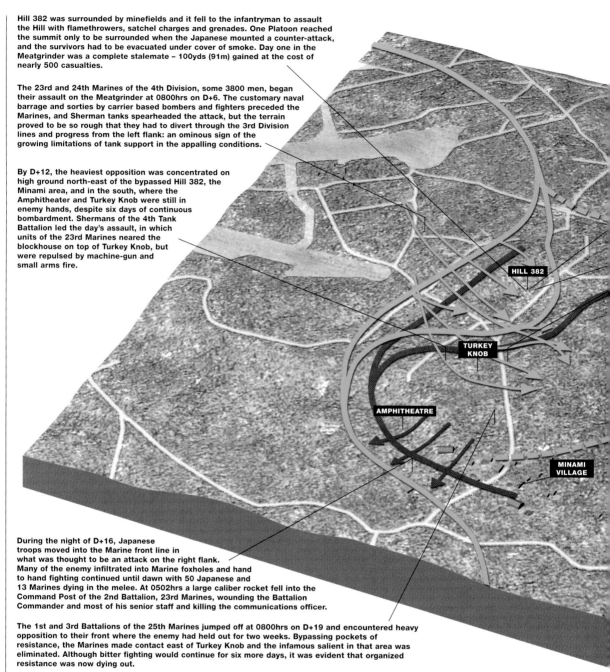

HILL 382

TURKEY KNOB

AMPHITHEATRE

MINAMI VILLAGE

During the night of D+16, Japanese troops moved into the Marine front line in what was thought to be an attack on the right flank. Many of the enemy infiltrated into Marine foxholes and hand to hand fighting continued until dawn with 50 Japanese and 13 Marines dying in the melee. At 0502hrs a large caliber rocket fell into the Command Post of the 2nd Battalion, 23rd Marines, wounding the Battalion Commander and most of his senior staff and killing the communications officer.

The 1st and 3rd Battalions of the 25th Marines jumped off at 0800hrs on D+19 and encountered heavy opposition to their front where the enemy had held out for two weeks. Bypassing pockets of resistance, the Marines made contact east of Turkey Knob and the infamous salient in that area was eliminated. Although bitter fighting would continue for six more days, it was evident that organized resistance was now dying out.

During the period when the 4th Division was pitted against the Meatgrinder, they were engaged in head-on assaults and fought a bloody path from Charlie Dog Ridge past Hill 382, the Amphitheater, Turkey Knob, through the ruins of Minami Village and almost to the east coast. The right flank, the hinge, advanced only 1000yds (914m), while the rest of the Division, the door, turned upon it and attacked north-east, east and south-east to close and sweep trapped enemy forces towards the sea.

ASSAULT ON THE MEATGRINDER D+6 – D+19

As Harry Schmidt's three Divisions fought slowly northward through Iwo Jima, the 4th Division came up against a complex of four formidable defense positions to the east of Airfield No2, that soon became known to the Marines as "The Meatgrinder". Defended by MajGen Senda's 2nd Mixed Brigade and elements of Baron Nish's 26th Tank Regiment, Hill 382, Turkey Knob, The Amphitheater and the ruins of Minami Village were to hold out until March 15 and be the scene of some of the bloodiest actions of the whole battle.

On D+7, Gen Cates alerted the 25th Marines to replace the battered 24th and three Battalions attacked behind an artillery barrage. Things went well for the first 100yds (91m) before a wall of extremely heavy machine-gun fire from the Amphitheater and Turkey Knob brought the advance to a grinding halt. The 23rd Marines on the left flank worked their way through a minefield and occupied a shattered radio station below Hill 382. On this day, Pfc Douglas Jacobson silenced sixteen strongpoints with his bazooka, killing 75 of the enemy and earning himself the Medal of Honor.

Moving out at dawn on D+12, Col Jordan's 24th Marines renewed the battle for Hill 382, while Col Wensinger's 23rd tackled the complex of Turkey Knob, the Amphitheater and Minami Village. Sherman tanks assigned to both units soon ground to a halt before an impenetrable wall of boulders, and as infantry moved against Turkey Knob, fire from the huge blockhouse on the summit stopped the advance in its tracks. The highlight of the day was the neutralization of Hill 382, now surrounded and of little strategic value.

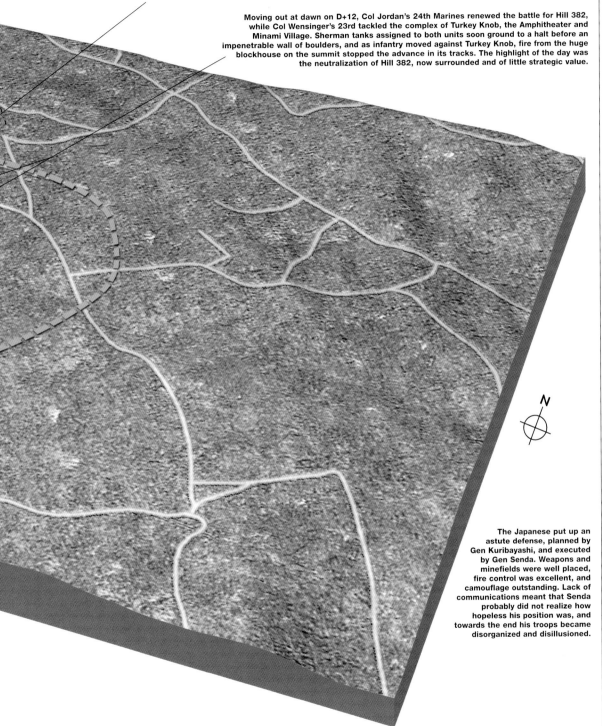

The Japanese put up an astute defense, planned by Gen Kuribayashi, and executed by Gen Senda. Weapons and minefields were well placed, fire control was excellent, and camouflage outstanding. Lack of communications meant that Senda probably did not realize how hopeless his position was, and towards the end his troops became disorganized and disillusioned.

53

The rocket trucks were prime targets for Japanese mortars and artillery. Here a Marine makes a dramatic exit as a barrage of mortar fire arrives near his truck. (National Archives)

D+9

The last day of February was to be a good one for the 3rd Division in the center of the island. Although this was the day that Harry Schmidt had predicted as the end of the battle, his orders for the day were for the 3rd to press forward towards the north coast. Relieving the battered 9th, the 21st Regiment moved out at 0900hrs and, under a huge naval and artillery barrage that appeared to have stunned the enemy, made good progress. At one point they were confronted by some of the few remaining "Ha-Go" tanks of Baron Nishi's 26th Regiment, but these flimsy vehicles were wiped out by bazookas and marauding aircraft leaving the Baron with only three serviceable tanks on the island. The Japanese soon recovered and by afternoon resistance had stiffened to such an extent that a second massive artillery barrage was called in and by 1300hrs the troops were again on the move. This time the momentum was maintained as the Marines stormed their way into the ruins of the village of Motoyama, once the largest settlement on Iwo Jima. The machine gunners and snipers who had taken over the ruins were soon ousted and Col Duplantis' 3rd Battalion swept on to occupy the high ground overlooking the unfinished Airfield No. 3.

As the 3rd Battalion advanced, the 1st and 2nd Battalions were busy dealing with the mass of overrun enemy positions and in an afternoon of grim fighting the flamethrowers and demolition teams secured the flanks. The flamethrower was the most practical weapon for clearing the enemy from caves, pillboxes, and bunkers. Horrific in its effect, it saved the lives of countless Marines who would otherwise have had to prise the enemy out in hand-to-hand fighting with an opponent who did not consider surrender an option. Pfc Hank Chamberlain describes an attack that was typical: "I was cover for a flamethrower near a row of caves. A grenade came flying out towards us and we dived behind an outcrop of rocks to our left and the grenade exploded harmlessly. The

A 155mm (6.1in) howitzer adds
its support to the 5th Division
barrage. (USMC)

flamethrower was now alongside the cave entrance and sidestepped in front of it and let off a long blast. A single Jap came tearing out. He was a mass of flames from head to foot and his shrieks were indescribable. Both Buckey and I had emptied our guns into the cave and we reloaded as fast as we could. The Jap was now writhing on the ground with his arms flaying the air. We put him out of his agony with enough bullets to kill a dozen men."

Over on the 5th Division front, the Marines were still confronted with Hill 362A – the top dotted with anti-tank guns and mortars, the slopes bristling with machine guns, and the base lined with bunkers and pillboxes. Two battalions of the 27th Regiment, supported by tanks, assaulted the hill with demolition charges and flamethrowers, but little progress was made and at 1200hrs six rocket firing trucks added salvos of 4.5in rockets. Some men reached the top but were driven back by determined enemy troops. The only gains of the day were made by the 1st Battalion who pushed back strong opposition to gain 300yds (274m) near the base.

The impasse at the "Meatgrinder" continued as the 4th Division continued to batter Hill 382 and "Turkey Knob." Attempts to encircle these positions were frustrated, and as smoke shells covered the withdrawal of forward troops, the operation was closed down for the day at 1645hrs.

The most memorable event of the day came at 1400hrs when a Japanese shell landed in a large ammunition dump near Airfield No. 1, and the whole of southern Iwo Jima erupted in a spectacular display of pyrotechnics. Shells exploded with a deafening bang, bullets popped and crackled, and huge clouds of smoke rolled out to sea. Miraculously there were no casualties, but the 5th Division lost almost a quarter of it stocks.

D+10

After a night overlooking Airfield No. 3, the 21st Regiment of the 3rd Division moved forward against surprisingly light resistance and by 1200hrs were across the main runway. Tanks rolled forward to stiffen the attack and all went well until the forward troops reached Hills 362B and

362C, two more heavily defended bastions barring the way to the coast, and the advance ran out of steam.

On the west coast, the 28th Regiment, the conquerors of Mount Suribachi, were now bolstering the 5th Division front as all three battalions were pitted against the complex of strongpoints north of Hill 362A. The day started with shelling by a battleship and three cruisers, and as the dust settled the 1st and 2nd Battalions stormed the slopes and reached the summit. The Japanese had abandoned the site through a labyrinth of caves and taken up new positions on Nishi Ridge, a ragged cliffline 200yds (183m) further north.

For the 4th Division, Hill 382 was the key to the impasse. Until it was taken the whole of the eastern side of Iwo Jima would be firmly in enemy hands, and in the pre-dawn darkness the 24th Regiment moved up to replace the 23rd. In a day of unremitting savagery the battle flowed back and forth. An early advance by the 1st and 2nd Battalions was stalled by a hail of mortar fire. The Japanese then took to their caves as a barrage from naval guns, artillery and carrier planes swept the area. As the 1st Battalion resumed the attack the enemy emerged from the depths and resumed their machine gun, mortar, and small arms fire from the high ground. By afternoon it was obvious that there was yet another stalemate.

The Generals were becoming increasingly concerned about the combat efficiency of their units. It was not unusual to see command pass from captain to lieutenant to sergeant and in some cases to Pfc (Private First Class). A confidential report of the 3rd Battalion 25th Regiment makes note of the situation at the front around this time: "Special note must here be made of the mental condition and morale of our troops. We have been in the assault for a period of ten days during which we

A couple of Marines utilize a captured Japanese Nambo machine gun as the fighting in the north intensifies. (National Archives)

Two flamethrowers, Pvt Richard Klatt on the left and Pfc Wildred Voegeli, demonstrate the terrifying effect of their weapons. (National Archives)

have shown a gain of approx. 800yds (732m). Initially, we had relieved troops whose position on the ground was far short of the position they showed themselves to occupy on the map. Throughout the assault we have suffered heavy casualties. One company commander and two platoon leaders have been killed in action. While it was true we did not move from D+11 to D+17, nevertheless throughout that period of time enemy mortar fire of various calibers fell in our zone of action inflicting many casualties. On D+8, without warning a strafing and napalm strike was made behind and within our lines although our front line panels were clearly displayed. On D+11, a TBF (Avenger Torpedo Bomber) accidentally dropped a lone bomb behind our lines. On D+12, without warning in any way, a rocket barrage, apparently from a rocket jeep, fell directly on our flank platoon. All of this contributed to make our troops "jittery." It is common knowledge that we were relieving a unit which had been unable to accomplish its mission."

General Erskine was scathing in his criticism of the quality of the replacements: "They get killed the day they go into battle," he said. The problem was the use of "battle replacements" as opposed to "organic replacements."

"Battle replacements were recruits who had gone through Parris Island in the summer of 1944, where they had fired for qualification once. In early September they were formed into an Infantry Training Unit at Camp Lejeune where they went through 'musketry range' once, threw one live grenade, fired one rifle grenade and went through one live fire exercise. Designated the 30th Replacement Draft in October, they went to Camp Pendleton and straight on to Maui in Hawaii where they worked on mess duties or working parties with no additional training. The day after Christmas Day they began boarding for Iwo Jima. Those who survived went back to Maui and began receiving the training that might have helped them before the operation," writes author and Iwo Jima veteran John Lane. The situation was typified by one replacement who was placed with a machine gun unit. When asked if he had any questions he replied, "Yes, how do you fire this thing?"

As the 5th Division advanced up the west coast, many enemy gun positions were captured. Here a Marine stands guard over a Japanese coastal artillery piece. (National Archives)

D+11

The pressure continued on Hill 382 and "Turkey Knob." The 1st Battalion of the 25th Regiment made pre-dawn infiltrations but were driven back by mortar shells raining down from the heights above. Sherman tanks and "Zippos" (flamethrower tanks) pounded the blockhouse on the top of "Turkey Knob" and the "Zippos" expended over 1,000 gallons of fuel on the caves, but the Japanese simply retired to the depths of their tunnels and sat out the inferno. Meanwhile the 26th Regiment, in some of the fiercest fighting of the day, secured a

Utilizing an enemy installation, Navy doctors perform front line surgery somewhere in the 4th Division sector. Note the doctor with scissors in his top pocket and kneepads. Conditions were primitive until the casualties could be evacuated. (National Archives)

foothold on the summit of Hill 382. Casualties were horrendous, one unit losing five officers in rapid succession –two fatally wounded, two seriously wounded and the other loosing his leg below the knee.

In the center, hopes of a dash to the north coast were fading. Although the sea was only 1,500yds (1372m) away the 3rd Division had yet to deal with Hills 362B and C. Four thousand men headed out in a two-pronged assault, one group headed for Hill 362B while the other deployed around Airfield No. 3. The approach to the hill was a flat area overlooked by artillery and offering virtually no cover. Tanks were brought forward and under their cover an advance of 500yds (457m) was made to the base of the hill.

On the right the 2nd Battalion moved towards the east of the airfield but made little progress as they came face to face with Baron Nishi's lines. Without his tanks the Baron was resigned to dying on the front line with the remains of his command. The glory days when he had won an Olympic medal on his horse Uranus and socialized with Los Angeles society and Hollywood stars were only a memory.

Colonel Chandler Johnson's 28th Regiment on the west coast were determined to secure Nishi Ridge. Advancing along the left side of Hill 363A they came under heavy fire but pushed on to the ravine between the hill and the ridge where they had a clear area from which the Shermans could blast the cliff face. Johnson, well known for being up front with his men, fell victim to what was probably a misplaced American round which blew him to pieces.

D+12 – D+19: DEADLOCK

D+12

Casualty figures were reaching epidemic proportions. By D+12 the Marine figure stood at 16,000 of whom more than 3,000 were dead. The Japanese numbers were staggering. Of the 21,000 troops in Gen Kuribayashi's command on D-Day, a mere 7,000 remained. The battle was dragging on far longer than the forecast of the Chiefs of Staff, deteriorating into an inexorable slog from gully to gully, ridge to ridge, and cave to cave.

The 5th Division kept up the pressure on the west coast as the 26th Regiment attacked Hill 362B (previously located in the 3rd Division sector but now re-allocated to the 5th), and the 28th Regiment confronted Nishi Ridge. In a grim day's fighting during which they suffered severe casualties, the 26th finally stormed to the top of Hill 362B although the enemy still occupied much of the surrounding area. But the best news of the day came with the capture of Nishi Ridge by the 28th Regiment, an achievement that pleased Gen Rockey who had envisaged a prolonged struggle for this strategically important location.

The 3rd Division again pitted themselves against the "Meatgrinder." Colonel Jordan's 24th Regiment renewed their assault on Hill 382 as Col Wensinger's 23rd tackled "Turkey Knob," the Amphitheater and Minami Village. Shermans of the 4th Tank Battalion had been assigned to both units, but the increasingly rocky terrain was taking its toll as a large proportion of the tanks ground to a halt before impenetrable mounds of rocks and boulders. Engineers braved heavy enemy fire in an

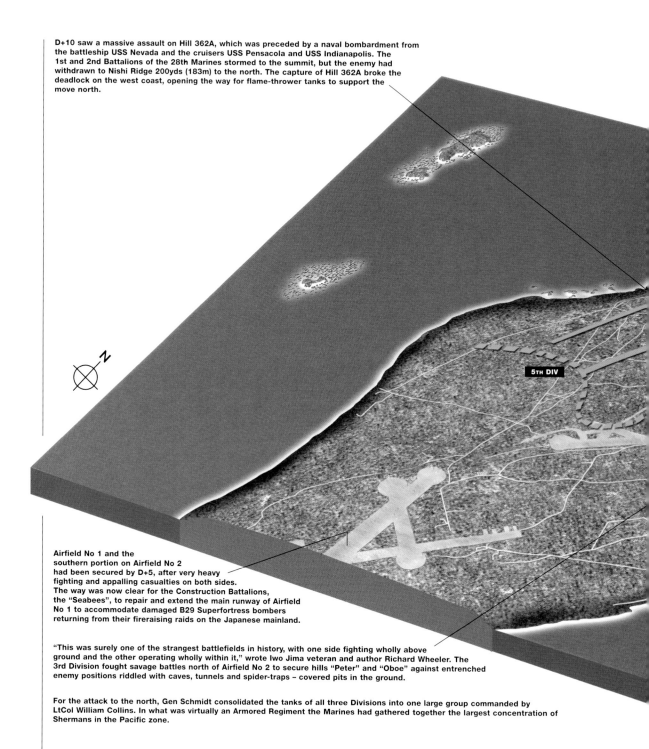

D+10 saw a massive assault on Hill 362A, which was preceded by a naval bombardment from the battleship USS Nevada and the cruisers USS Pensacola and USS Indianapolis. The 1st and 2nd Battalions of the 28th Marines stormed to the summit, but the enemy had withdrawn to Nishi Ridge 200yds (183m) to the north. The capture of Hill 362A broke the deadlock on the west coast, opening the way for flame-thrower tanks to support the move north.

5TH DIV

Airfield No 1 and the southern portion on Airfield No 2 had been secured by D+5, after very heavy fighting and appalling casualties on both sides. The way was now clear for the Construction Battalions, the "Seabees", to repair and extend the main runway of Airfield No 1 to accommodate damaged B29 Superfortress bombers returning from their fireraising raids on the Japanese mainland.

"This was surely one of the strangest battlefields in history, with one side fighting wholly above ground and the other operating wholly within it," wrote Iwo Jima veteran and author Richard Wheeler. The 3rd Division fought savage battles north of Airfield No 2 to secure hills "Peter" and "Oboe" against entrenched enemy positions riddled with caves, tunnels and spider-traps – covered pits in the ground.

For the attack to the north, Gen Schmidt consolidated the tanks of all three Divisions into one large group commanded by LtCol William Collins. In what was virtually an Armored Regiment the Marines had gathered together the largest concentration of Shermans in the Pacific zone.

THE ATTACK NORTH D+5 - D+16

Mount Suribachi, with it's commanding views over most of Iwo Jima, was now secure and MajGen Harry Schmidt, the V Amphibious Corps Commander, planned to attack the Japanese on a broad front with his three Divisions abreast – the 5th in the west, the 3rd in the center, and the 4th in the east. It immediately became apparent that the Marines had reached Gen Kuribayashi's main defense belt, and the fighting degenerated into small unit actions of incredible savagery.

On D+15 the Navy and Marines produced the heaviest bombardment of the battle. Marine artillery expended 22500 rounds in 67 minutes working across the Japanese lines from west to east. The Navy battleships, cruisers and destroyers lobbed 14in (356mm) and 8in (203mm) shells into known enemy strongpoints and Corsair and Dauntless fighters and bombers attacked with bombs and napalm cannisters for over one hour. The pounding appeared to have little effect and only marginal progress was achieved.

In the northern sector of the 3rd Division zone all the high-ground north-east of Airfield No 3 had been seized by D+12 after harrowing close-quarter fighting, and Gen Erskine ordered the 9th Regiment to advance against Hill 357 in an attempt to reach the north coast and split the enemy forces through the middle of the island.

By D+16 Marine casualties stood at 2777 dead and 8051 wounded and Gen Schmidt was a worried man. At 0500hrs the 3rd Battalion of the 9th Regiment, 3rd Division silently advanced towards Hill 362C – the last obstacle between the Marines and the sea. The enemy counter-attacked at 0530hrs, but the objective was secured by 1400hrs after heavy fighting, and with the coast only 800yds (732m) beyond the front line there was an excellent prospect of splitting the enemy down the middle.

3RD DIV

APPROX. FRONT LINE. D+16

APPROX. FRONT LINE. D+5

4TH DIV

Near the east coast the 23rd and 24th Regiments of the 4th Division deployed to the east and then swung south, trapping around 1500 troops of Gen Senda and Navy Capt Inouye between them and the 25th Regiment. Strictly against Gen Kuribayashi's orders, Inouye opted for a night-time "banzai" attack, and around midnight they advanced towards the Marine front line. By the light of star shells, the Japanese died in their hundreds under a barrage of artillery, machine-gun and small arms fire.

The advance on D+6 brought the 4th Division face to face with a complex of formidable positions defended by MajGen Senda's 2nd Mixed Brigade and elements of Baron Nishi's 26th Tank Regiment (now devoid of tanks). Hill 382 to the east of the main east-west runway was peppered with caves and pillboxes, the "Amphitheater": a bowl-shaped depression bristling with artillery and mortar positions, and "Turkey Knob": a hill surmounted by a huge blockhouse – here was a complex 600yds (549m) diameter killing ground that the Marines were to aptly name "The Meatgrinder".

With Airfield No 1 now fully operational, the first B29 Superfortress bomber to land on Iwo Jima was able to put down. With bomb bays jammed in the open position and a malfunctioning fuel tank valve, "Dinah Might" was the first of many bombers to make emergency landings on the island. General Paul Tibbets, pilot of the "Enola Gay", estimated that over 22000 aircrew owed their lives to the valor of the Marines in securing the island.

The Superfortress "Dinah Might" was the first B29 to land on the island. The arrival attracted a great deal of attention, as crowds of Marines and Seabees gathered to see the huge bomber. (National Archives)

attempt to clear a path but with little success. As the 24th Regiment advanced they were confronted by a nest of concrete pillboxes but, with the help of the few tanks that had broken through, surrounded Hill 382. This was to be the only significant gain of the day as the 23rd came to a grinding halt from enfilading fire from the remaining positions.

Although the day had been disappointing in material gains it had been one of incredible valor, five Medals of Honor being awarded for acts of heroism that almost defy belief. Two Marines died saving the lives of their companions by throwing themselves onto hand grenades. Two Corpsmen enhanced the reputation of the Navy medics by outstanding acts of self-sacrifice. One ministered to the wounded until he had to be dragged to the rear to have his own life-threatening wounds attended to, and the other died as he refused aid so that he could continue tending wounded Marines. The fifth, Sgt William Harrell, won his medal defending his front line position against nighttime infiltrators, suffering horrific wounds including the loss of both hands.

D+13

In deteriorating weather, icy drizzle, and leaden clouds, carrier plane sorties and naval bombardments were called off because of poor visibility. An overall weariness seemed to permeate the entire front as the Marines battled with a seemingly invisible enemy which spent most of its daylight hours in their caves and tunnels, emerging at night to infiltrate the American line, more intent on foraging for food and water than killing the enemy.

In the knowledge that the battle was swinging irrevocably in favor of the Americans, Gen Kuribayashi radioed Tokyo: "Our strongpoints might be able to fight delaying actions for several more days. I comfort myself a little seeing my officers and men die without regret after struggling in this inch-by-inch battle against an overwhelming enemy …". The General's predictions were, if anything, on the pessimistic side as his garrison would prolong the battle for another three weeks.

As tanks and rocket launchers pounded the Amphitheater in the east, the 3rd Division in the center were unable to make any significant progress. In the west the 5th Division continued to engage the more exposed positions with flamethrowers and grenades, but little progress could be reported over the entire front. A communiqué at 1700hrs from the Command Posts of Generals Rockey, Erskine, and Cates: "There will be no general attack tomorrow … Divisions will utilise the day for rest, refitting, and re-organization in preparation for resumption of action on March 6." It was clear that the Marines desperately needed a break after two weeks of the bloodiest fighting the Corps had ever experienced.

The highlight of the day was the arrival of "Dinah Might," the first B29 Superfortress bomber to land on Iwo Jima. With bomb bays jammed in the open position and problems with the fuel transfer valve, the aircraft had struggled back from a mission south-west of Tokyo. As she ground to a halt at the northern end of the main runway on Airfield No. 1, the Japanese directed a steady hail of artillery fire in the general direction, causing the huge plane to swing around and retire rapidly to the Mount Suribachi end of the airfield. The bloody sacrifices of the Marine Corps in securing the island were beginning to pay dividends in the lives of what were to be thousands of Air Force crewmen.

D+14

The day was one of "consolidation, replenishment, and rest." Unfortunately, no one had informed the Japanese who continued to lob artillery rounds and mortar shells into the Marine lines all day. Tank crews serviced their machines; ammunition, food, and fresh water were brought to the front; hot coffee and doughnuts arrived from the newly

As the battle moved further north, the terrain became increasingly difficult. Here a group examine an abandoned Japanese car among a mass of boulders and rocks. (National Archives)

installed bakery in the rear, and replacements filtered through to relieve many of the exhausted troops who had slogged for fourteen days in hell.

With undue optimism the Navy began to run down its support. Admiral Spruance in his flagship USS *Indianapolis* departed for Guam, along with the 3rd Regiment of the 3rd Division, seasoned troops that Harry Schmidt would have preferred to the green replacements from Hawaii. However, there were some newcomers. Army units who were to garrison Iwo Jima after the departure of the Marines began to disembark, and the first of the Mustang and Black Widow fighters took their places on the handstands of the airfield

D+15

If the Generals had hoped that the day of rest and replenishment would mean big advances on Tuesday they were to be bitterly disappointed.

The Navy and Marine artillery mounted one of the heaviest bombardments of the battle and within 67 minutes the artillery fired 22,500 rounds. A battleship, a cruiser, and three destroyers added a further 450 rounds of 14in and 8in shells, while Dauntless and Corsair carrier planes strafed and dropped bombs and napalm canisters.

Between 0800hrs and 0900hrs the 4th and 5th Divisions moved forward but resistance was as fierce as ever. The 21st and 27th Regiments on the west coast were halted by shredding machine gun and mortar fire before they had gone more than a few yards, and support from "Zippo" flamethrower tanks had little effect. Marine Dale Worley wrote: "They have almost blown Hill 362 off the map. There are bodies everywhere and the ground is spotted with blood. The smell is sickening."

In the center the 3rd Division made little progress. One element of the 21st Regiment, under Lt Mulvey, battered their way to the top of yet another ridge and saw before them the prize that had so long eluded them – the sea. He estimated that it was less than a quarter of a mile away and called for reinforcements. A dozen men came forward but before they could reach the Lieutenant six were killed and two wounded, and the group had to retire under a storm of enemy fire. In the east the best advance of the day was a mere 350yds (320m) by the 3rd Battalion of the 24th Regiment aided by four "Zippo" flamethrower tanks.

D+16

General Erskine had, for a long while, been toying with the idea of a night attack. As a veteran of World War I he had witnessed many such actions and was aware that the Japanese knew that the Marines usually confined their fighting to daytime. His plan was to infiltrate the enemy lines for about 250yds (229m) and capture Hill 362C, the last major obstacle between the 3rd Division and the sea.

At 0500hrs the 3rd Battalion of the 9th Regiment under the command of LtCol Harold Boehm moved silently forward and for thirty minutes their luck held until an alert enemy machine gunner opened up on their left. Pressing forward, Boehm and his men stormed to the top of the hill and radioed back to Erskine who said: "We caught the bastards asleep just as we thought we would." But the euphoria was short lived, as Boehm checked his maps and realised that he was atop Hill 331 and not 362C. In the darkness and driving rain, one Iwo Jima hill looked much like another. Calling in artillery support, Boehm and his battalion

pushed forward despite heavy opposition from the front and both flanks, and by 1400hrs finally reached the correct objective.

As he was moving towards Hill 362C, the 1st and 2nd Battalions were advancing on his right flank, but soon encountered heavy resistance from their front and from bypassed positions. LtCol Cushman and his 2nd Battalion had stumbled across the remains of Baron Nishi's Tank Regiment and soon found themselves surrounded. It was not until the next day that the remains of Cushman's battalion could be extricated with the aid of tanks. Bitter fighting was to continue in this area for another six days in what was to become known as "Cushman's Pocket."

On the 5th Division front, the 26th Regiment, approaching a ridge just north of the ruins of Nishi Village, found the enemy opposition to be almost nonexistent. Cautiously proceeding to the summit they expected a fusillade of fire from the far side as had often happened in the past. Instead, the whole ridge disappeared in a massive explosion that could be heard for miles around. The Japanese had mined their Command Post and it was left to the Marines to recover the bodies of 43 of their comrades.

In a clever maneuver in the 4th Division sector, the 23rd and 24th Regiments moved to the east and then swung sharply south, edging the Japanese towards the 25th Regiment which had assumed a defensive line. Realizing that they were trapped, Gen Senda and Navy Capt Inouye, with 1,500 men, elected for a "banzai" attack, strictly against the instructions of Gen Kuribayashi. At around 2400hrs a large column of men armed with grenades, small arms, swords, and bamboo spears moved south in a bizarre attempt to infiltrate the American lines, scale Mount Suribachi and raise the Japanese flag. Caught in the nightly display of flares provided by offshore destroyers, the column was decimated by artillery and machine gun fire. The morning light was to reveal scores of bodies littering the area.

The story of Inouye's "banzai" attack was revealed years later by two of his orderlies who survived and were captured. Many of his troops

Corpsmen and stretcher-bearers evacuate some of the wounded to landing craft on the beach, from where they went either to offshore LVTs or to hospital ships. (National Archives)

believed that Inouye was a superior leader who inspired his men to perform outstanding feats of bravery – others thought he was a maniac. The sight of the Stars and Stripes flying on top of Mount Suribachi had filled him with increasing rage. He is quoted as saying: "We shall destroy their banner, we shall replace it with ours in the name of the great Emperor and the great people of Japan."

Inouye was in charge of the Naval Guard Force who manned the shore guns that sank and damaged many of the US warships and landing craft, and was described as a bombastic and temperamental character, a fine swordsman, heavy drinker, and womanizer. His bizarre plan almost beggars belief. The Captain was certain that the airfields would be lightly defended by service troops. He and his men would move southward, destroying B29 bombers as they passed; climb Mount Suribachi and tear down the Stars and Stripes; and replace it with the Rising Sun as an inspiration to all Japanese troops on the island.

General Sendra radioed Kuribayashi to seek approval for the attack but the General was furious and declared it impractical and stupid. Sendra and Inouye consulted and decided to go ahead anyway. As night fell, the Marines of the 23rd and 24th Regiments became aware of increasing activity in the enemy lines. First voices, and after about two hours, a barrage of artillery fire thundered across the front line as large numbers of Japanese troops began to infiltrate the American lines. Some, probably the officers, wielded sabres, a few had machine guns, most had rifles and grenades, and some of the sailors carried crude wooden spears or had demolition charges strapped to their chests. In the chaos that followed, the Marines fired flares and star shells to illuminate the sky as they shredded the onrushing enemy with machine gun fire, rifles, and 60mm (2.36in) mortars. Some of the Japanese wore Marine helmets, others shouted "Corpsman" in English and throughout the night bitter hand-to-hand struggles and grenade-throwing contests erupted all along the line. The morning revealed the extent of the carnage. A body count showed almost 800 Japanese dead, probably the largest number of casualties that they suffered in a single day and a justification of Gen Kuribayashi's reluctance to sanction the attack. Marine casualties were 90 dead and 257 wounded.

D+17

March 9 saw two more Marines earn the Medal of Honor. Nineteen year old Pfc James LaBelle flung himself on a spluttering grenade and died saving the lives of his two companions, while in a push up the west coast towards Kitano Point, Lt Jack Lummus silenced two enemy emplacements and then ran ahead of his men urging them forward. As he did he stepped on a mine and both his legs were blown off. When the dust and debris settled, his men were amazed to see him still standing on his bloody stumps waving them on. Lummus died that afternoon in the 3rd Division hospital from shock and loss of blood.

The day saw steady if unspectacular progress. Cushman's Pocket still barred the progress of the 3rd Division, and the 4th were still confronted with "Turkey Knob" and the Amphitheater.

D+18

The final breakthrough to the sea was achieved by a 28-man patrol led by Lt Paul Connally. As the men swilled their faces in the icy water, mortar rounds began falling among them and there was a mad scramble back to the safety of the cliffs. Connally had filled his water bottle with sea water and passed it back to his CO, Col Withers, who in turn sent it to Gen Erskine with the message "for inspection, not consumption."

With the battle now confined to the north of the island, the Divisional cemeteries were established. The 5th Division cemetery is flanked on the left by that of the 3rd Division and on the right, the 4th Division; Mount Suribachi looms in the distance. (USMC)

FIFTH MARINE DIVISION

That same night, as the Marines bedded down after another frustrating day which saw only minor gains on the 4th and 5th Division fronts, the drone of hundreds of aircraft was heard as they skirted the east of Iwo Jima. Three hundred and twenty-five B29s from Saipan, Tinian, and Guam were heading for Tokyo for the first of Gen Curtis

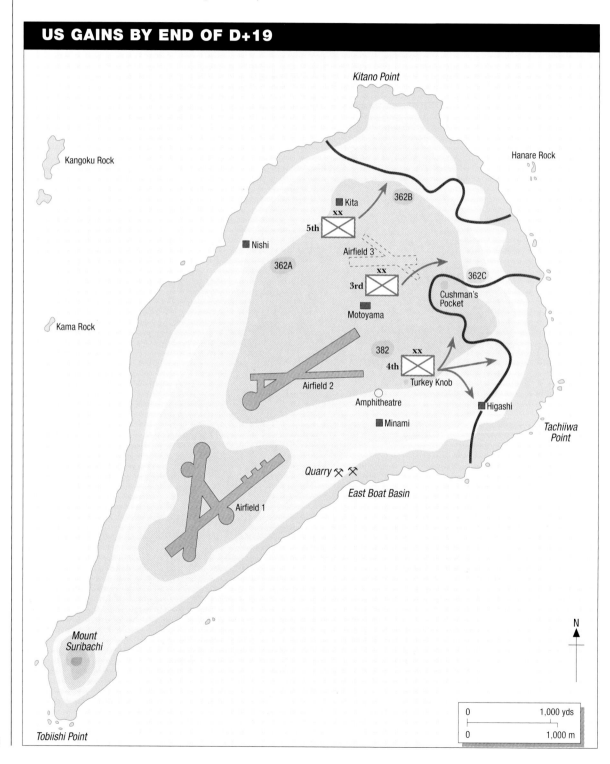

US GAINS BY END OF D+19

LeMay's "fire raising" raids. In a dramatic change in policy, daylight precision bombing had been abandoned in favor of "area bombing" which had been practiced by the RAF against Germany since 1941. In a spectacular raid that destroyed almost a quarter of Tokyo and killed 83,793 people, LeMay had spelled out his intentions for the future of the 20th Air Force's assault against the Japanese mainland.

D+19

It was obvious to both sides that, by March 10, the battle was reaching its climax. Cushman's Pocket was proving a tough nut to crack and the "Meatgrinder" and "Turkey Knob" were still to be taken. However, the Japanese were nearing the end of their endurance as diminishing numbers, chronic shortages of ammunition, food, and water were taking their toll. In the north-west corner of the island Gen Kuribayashi prepared his final enclave, one which was significantly to be called "Death Valley" by the Marines. Located about 500yds (457m) south of Kitano Point, it was a nightmare of rocks, caves and gullies where the 1,500 remaining troops prepared for the end. The General informed Tokyo: "The enemy's bombardments are very severe, so fierce that I cannot express or write it here. The troops are still fighting bravely and holding their positions thoroughly."

D+20 – D+36: "GOODBYE FROM IWO"

The Japanese were now confined to three distinct areas: one was Cushman's Pocket, the second an area on the east coast between the village of Higashi and the sea, and the other was Death Valley on the north-west coast where Gen Kuribayashi and the remains of his command were entrenched. Conventional battle was abandoned as the infantry slugged it out with a desperate enemy. Tanks could only operate in the few areas where bulldozers could clear a path for them. Artillery fire was reduced dramatically as the front lines merged, and many gunners found themselves donning combat gear. The heavy elements of the Navy

This photograph dramatically shows the type of terrain in which the final phase of the battle was fought. Every rock and boulder could hide a sniper; tank warfare was impossible; the fighting descended into a hand-to-hand slog between opposing infantrymen. (USMC)

Prisoners were rare on Iwo Jima. A group of curious Marines stop to stare at one of the few Japanese taken alive. (National Archives)

departed for Guam, and the Mustangs took over from the carrier aircraft in providing ground support with bombs, rockets and napalm.

In a cynical move to placate public alarm at the mounting casualty figures released by the War Department, Iwo Jima was declared "secure" on March 14. In a ceremony held in the shadow of Mount Suribachi, Harry Schmidt's personnel officer read the statement as an artillery barrage thundered in the north of the island, almost drowning out his words. The irony of the situation was obvious to all.

In the north-west, the 5th Division regrouped and re-armed in preparation for the final assault on Gen Kuribayashi's headquarters in Death Valley (or "The Gorge" as the Marine maps labeled it). Meanwhile the 3rd Division fought a bloody battle in Cushman's Pocket, slowly grinding down the fanatical remnants of Baron Nishi's command. The Baron, partially blinded in the fighting, held out until the end using dug-in tanks as artillery and fighting from a maze of caves until the Pocket finally fell silent. The Baron's fate is uncertain as his body was never identified and none of his staff survived.

General Senda, who had declined to take part in the mad "banzai" attack of D+16, was still holding out in an area east of Higashi. Prisoners estimated his strength at around 300 men, and in an attempt to reduce the carnage, Gen Erskine arranged for loudspeakers to broadcast to the

Japanese to explain the futility of further resistance. However, the equipment failed to work and his efforts were in vain. The slaughter continued four more days until the whole garrison were eliminated. The body of General Senda was never found.

With only Death Valley to secure, Harry Schmidt could be forgiven for thinking that the battle was all but over. He sadly misjudged Kuribayashi, and another ten days of savage fighting and 1,724 casualties lay ahead. Death Valley was around 700yds (640m) long and between 300 (274m) and 500yds (457m) wide with dozens of canyons and gullies leading off on both sides. In a cave somewhere in this labyrinth the General planned his final stand.

Colonel Liversedge's 28th Regiment moved up the coast and took up their positions on the cliffs overlooking the Valley, while the remainder of the division attacked from the center and from the east. In a week of attrition the Marines painfully squeezed the Japanese further and further back until, by March 24, the enemy had been reduced to an area of around 50yds (46m) square. Flamethrower tanks had expended over 10,000 gallons of fuel per day burning out caves and crevices. So badly mauled was the 2nd Battalion that they ceased to exist as a fighting force, and the 1st Battalion was on its third commander in nine days. The first was decapitated, the second maimed by a mine, and the third lost his left arm to a burst of machine gun fire.

Again Gen Erskine tried to persuade the enemy to give up the hopeless struggle, sending Japanese POWs and Nisei (Japanese Americans) to contact the defenders. General Kuribayashi, in radio contact with Major Horie on Chichi Jima, said: "We only laughed at this childish trick and did not set ourselves against them." On March 17, Horie had contacted the General informing him of his promotion to full General, and on the evening of March 23 received a final message: "All officers and men of Chichi Jima, – goodbye from Iwo."

In the pre-dawn darkness of March 26, the final act of the tragedy was performed. Between 200 and 300 Japanese troops from Death Valley and other scattered positions on the west coast silently crept through the ravines of the 5th Division sector headed for a tented area between Airfield No. 2 and the sea occupied by a mixture of Seabees, Air Force personnel, Shore Parties and AA Gunners. Most of them were sleeping, secure in the knowledge that the battle was virtually over. In a three-pronged attack they slashed tents, stabbed sleeping men, threw grenades, and fired pistols and rifles at the hapless sleepers. The noise soon alerted troops from the surrounding area, and Marines from a nearby Pioneer Battalion, Negro troops from a Shore Party, and soldiers from the 147th Infantry joined battle in a frenzy of shooting, punching, kicking and stabbing. Dawn revealed the full extent of the carnage in the ruined encampment: 44 Airman and 9 Marines lay dead with a further 119 wounded; of the attackers 262 were killed and 18 captured. Lt Harry Martin of the 5th Pioneers had hurriedly organized a defense line during the attack and single-handedly killed four enemy machine gunners before dying himself. He was to be Iwo Jima's final Medal of Honor hero, bringing the total to an incredible 27.

The circumstances of Gen Kuribayashi's death have always been shrouded in mystery. Over the years various sources have suggested that he died in the fighting around Death Valley or that he killed himself in

The thousands of Japanese dead that were found throughout the north of Iwo Jima were collected in tractors and unceremoniously dumped in any convenient shell hole or pit. (USMC)

The handsome and dashing LtCol (Baron) Nishi, commander of the 26th Tank Regiment, was something of a legend in Japan. He had won a gold medal in the equestrian event at the 1932 Olympic Games in Los Angeles, and was a member of a very wealthy and influential family with links to the Emperor. Around D+20, in Cushman's Pocket, the Baron and the remains of his command were resisting strongly from a complex of caves as the 5th Division began the final onslaught. Partially blinded, the Baron and his men held out for longer than most until the Pocket fell silent. Some say that he was killed leading a raid, others that he committed hara-kiri. The exact nature of his death will never be known.

his HQ. In a letter to the author, his son Taro offers the following version, which is probably the more authoritative: "It seems that it was after sunset on March 25 to the dawn of the 26th that surviving Imperial Japanese forces were obliged to stand still under the US onslaught and showering shells. Under such circumstances, he had his sword in his left hand and ordered the chief staff officer, Col Takaishi, who was beside him, 'Send snipers to shoot' (Sgt Oyama heard the order.). Oyama, who was seriously wounded in the last combat, fell unconscious, was hospitalized by the US and after having served as a POW came back and testified the dreadful account of the night to me. My father had believed it shameful to have his body discovered by the enemy even after death, so he had previously asked his two soldiers to come along with him, one in front and the other behind, with a shovel in hand. In case of his death he had wanted them to bury his body there and then. It seems that my father and the soldiers were killed by shells, and he was buried at the foot of a tree in Chidori Village, along the beach near Osaka Mountain. Afterwards Gen Smith spent a whole day looking for his body to pay respect accordingly and to perform a burial, but in vain."

What is without doubt is that he proved to be Japan's greatest wartime general and in Holland Smith's opinion: "Our most redoubtable adversary."

A memorial stands near the site of General Kuribayashi's cave in Death Valley. (Taro Kuribayashi)

AFTERMATH

Operation Detachment was planned and executed in accordance with the necessities of the time. Iwo Jima posed a major threat to the 20th Air Force's campaign against the Japanese mainland and its occupation was imperative as subsequent statistics proved. A total of 2,251 B29 Superfortress bombers made forced landings on the island during and after the battle. This represented 24,761 crewmen who would otherwise have had to ditch in the 1,300-mile expanse of ocean between Japan and the Marianas with a minimal chance of survival.

In an interview with the author, General Paul Tibbets, pilot of the Superfortress "Enola Gay" which dropped the Hiroshima bomb says: "On March 4, 1945, when the first B29 in distress landed on Iwo Jima, until the end of the war, more than 2,200 aircraft made emergency landings on Iwo. Many wounded crewmen on board would not have made the return trip to their home bases. Had it not been for the heroic valor of the Marines in securing the island and the Navy Seabees who built the runways, more than 22,000 pilots and air crew would have perished in crash landings at sea."

The B29 Superfortress "Enola Gay" (named after the pilot's mother) with Colonel Paul Tibbets, its pilot. The atomic bombing of Hiroshima and Nagasaki brought the war to an end. Few Marines have any regrets about the events and consider that they owe their lives to the bombings. (Paul Tibbets)

The capture of the Philippine Islands and the invasion of Okinawa in April accelerated the pace of the war. The 20th Air Force fire raising raids and the dropping of the atomic bombs on Hiroshima and Nagasaki ended it, and the island of Iwo Jima, secured at a terrible cost in Marine lives, played a major role in these events.

Since the end of the war many revisionists have condemned the dropping of the atomic bombs as acts of terrorism against helpless civilians; few have considered the alternative. Operation Downfall, the invasion of the Japanese mainland by the Marine Corps and the US Army, was already planned and filled the Government, Army, and USMC with foreboding. Knowing the ethos of fanatical commitment to Emperor and country that was prevalent at that time, and drawing from experience gleaned at Saipan, Iwo Jima, and Okinawa, the military knew that every beach, town, village, and field would be defended to the death by both the armed forces and the civilian population.

Japan still had 2,350,000 regular troops, 250,000 garrison troops, 7,000 aircraft, 4,000,000 employees of the armed services and 23,000,000 men, women, boys and girls sworn to fight to the death. Adding the kamikazes and the remnants of the navy provided the ingredients for a bloodbath that would make previous battles pale into insignificance. The Joint Chiefs were expecting 70 percent casualties in the landing force and the war was projected to last until 1946 or even 1947. Troops, ships, and aircraft (Tiger Force) were already on their way from the European theater when the war ended. The author, who has corresponded and talked to hundreds of Marine veterans, has yet to meet one who does not consider that he owes his life to the dropping of those bombs.

IWO JIMA TODAY

Evidence of the battle remains around this cave entrance with the mass of bullet holes. (Taro Kuribayashi)

With the exception of Pearl Harbor on the Hawaiian island of Oahu, the majority of the Pacific World War II battlefields are remote, and difficult and expensive to visit. In the case of Iwo Jima it is almost impossible.

After the war the US Air Force maintained a base on the island for twenty years and a US Coast Guard contingent remained until 1968 to operate the LORAN (Long Range Aid to Navigation) station situated near Kitano Point in the north. This token presence vanished in 1993 when the island was turned over to the Japanese Maritime Safety Agency and Iwo Jima was returned to Japanese jurisdiction and is now a government installation and a national war memorial. With no visitor facilities or civilian airport the only access for westerners is via the annual one-day trips, organized by Marine Corps oriented tour companies, which are almost exclusively allocated to Iwo Jima veterans.

All American dead were removed prior to the handover and re-interred in either the Punchbowl Cemetery in Hawaii or returned to the United States. No such service could be provided for the Japanese dead most of whom were either buried in mass graves or sealed in caves and tunnels during the battle. For many years groups of "bone diggers" from Japan, led by Tsuenzo Wachi, former Imperial Navy Captain and one time commander on Iwo Jima, returned to recover the remains of the garrison.

The island now bears little resemblance to the wartime battlefield. The three airfields have been replaced by one huge north to south runway with adjacent hangers and living quarters. Once-familiar locations like Cushman's Pocket, Nishi Ridge, the Quarry, the "Meatgrinder" and Motoyama Village have vanished under the bulldozer, and Mount Suribachi is studded with monuments. Only the landing beaches with their familiar black ash are tangible reminders, for the veterans who make their pilgrimages, of the carnage that took place here more than half a century ago.

CHRONOLOGY

1941

December 7	Japanese attack Pearl Harbor. US declares war on Japan.
December 8	Japanese assault Philippines, Hong Kong, Malaya and Wake Island.
December 11	Germany and Italy declare war on the United States.

1942

February 15	Singapore falls to Gen Yamashita.
March 12	General MacArthur leaves Philippines vowing "I shall return."
May 6	All US forces in Philippines surrender.
May 7	Battle of the Coral Sea – first Japanese setback of the war.
June 4–7	Battle of Midway – Japanese lose four carriers; turning point of the Pacific War.
August 7	US Marines land on Guadalcanal in Solomon Islands.

1943

February 1	All Japanese troops evacuate Guadalcanal.
June 30	Operation Cartwheel – operations against remainder of Solomon Islands.
November 20-23	Battle of Tarawa – start of Marines "island hopping" operations.

1944

February 2	Marines assault Kwajalein in Marshall Islands.
June 11	US Task Force 58 bombards Mariana Islands.
June 15	Invasion of Marianas begins at Saipan.
June 19	Battle of the Philippine Sea – destruction of Japanese naval air power.
August 8	Island of Guam in Marianas occupied.
September 15	1st Marine Division assault Peleliu in Palau Islands.
October 20	US Army under MacArthur land on Leyte in Philippines.
November 27	B29 Superfortress bombers firebomb Tokyo.

1945

February 19	Three Marine divisions assault Iwo Jima.
March 26 - June 30	Battle of Okinawa.
August 6	Atomic bomb dropped on Hiroshima.
September 2	Japanese surrender aboard USS *Missouri* in Tokyo Bay.

SELECT BIBLIOGRAPHY

Alexander, Col Joseph *Closing In – Marines in the Seizure of Iwo Jima*,
    Marine Corps Historical Center (Washington, DC, 1994)
Alexander, Col Joseph *A Fellowship of Valor*, HarperCollins (New York, 1997)
Bartley, LtCol Whitman S *Iwo Jima, Amphibious Epic*,
    USMC Official History 1954.
    Reprinted by Battery Press (Nashville, Tennessee, 1988)
Lane, John *This Here is G Company*, Bright Lights Publications
    (Great Neck, NY, 1997)
Newcomb, Richard F *Iwo Jima*, Holt, Rinehart & Winston (New York, 1965)
Ross, Bill D *Iwo Jima – Legacy of Valor*, Random House (New York, 1985)
Vat, Dan van der *The Pacific Campaign*, Simon & Schuster (New York, 1991)
Waterhouse Col Charles *Marines and Others*, Sea Bag Productions
    (Edison, NJ, 1994)
Wells, John Keith *Give Me 50 Marines Not Afraid to Die*,
    Quality Publications (1995)
Wheeler, Richard *Iwo*, Lippincott & Crowell (New York, 1980)
Wright, Derrick *The Battle for Iwo Jima 1945*, Sutton Publishing,
    (Slough, Glos., 1999)

APPENDICES

APPENDIX NO. 1

US COMMAND AND STAFF LIST

Expeditionary Troops (TF 56)
Commanding General   LtGen Holland M. Smith

V Amphibious Corps (VACLF)
Commanding General   MajGen Harry Schmidt

3rd Marine Division
Commanding General   MajGen Graves B. Erskine

3rd Regiment   Col James A. Stuart

(This regiment did not land on Iwo Jima and did not actively participate in that operation.
The 3rd Reg. remained in the area as Ex Trp Pac Reserve until March 5, 1945, when it returned to Guam.)

9th Regiment   Col Howard N. Kenyon
  1st Battalion   LtCol Cary A. Randell
  2nd   "   LtCol Robert E. Cushman
  3rd   "   LtCol Harold C. Boehm

21st Regiment   Col Hartnoll J Withers
  1st Battalion   LtCol Marlowe Williams
  2nd   "   LtCol Lowell E. English
  3rd   "   LtCol Wendell H. Duplantis

4th Marine Division
Commanding General   MajGen Clifton B. Cates

23rd Regiment   Col Walter W. Wensinger
  1st Battalion   LtCol Ralph Haas
  2nd   "   Maj Robert H. Davidson
  3rd   "   Maj James S. Scales

24th Regiment   Col Walter I. Jordan
  1st Battalion   Maj Paul S. Treitel
  2nd   "   LtCol Richard Rothwell
  3rd   "   LtCol Alexander A. Vandegrift, Jr.

25th Regiment   Col John R. Lanigan
  1st Battalion   LtCol Hollis U. Mustain
  2nd   "   LtCol Lewis C. Hudson, Jr.
  3rd   "   LtCol Justice M. Chambers

5th Marine Division

Commanding General   MajGen Keller E. Rockey

26th Regiment.   Col Chester B. Graham
  1st Battalion.   LtCol Daniel C. Pollock
  2nd   "   LtCol Joseph P. Sayers
  3rd   "   LtCol Tom M. Trotti

27th Regiment.   Col Thomas A. Wornham
  1st Battalion.   LtCol John A. Butler
  2nd   "   Maj John W. Antonelli
  3rd   "   LtCol Donn J. Robertson

28th Regiment.   Col Harry B. Liversedge
  1st Battalion.   LtCol Jackson B. Butterfield
  2nd   "   LtCol Chandler W. Johnson
  3rd   "   LtCol Charles E. Shepard, Jr.

Of the battalion commanders who landed on D-Day, only seven remained unwounded
and in command at the end of the battle.

US Task Force Organization

Overall Command of Iwo Jima Operation   Adm Raymond A. Spruance
Task Force 51 (Joint Expeditionary Force)   V/Adm Richmond K. Turner
Task Force 52 (Amphibious Support Force)   R/Adm William H. P. Blandy
Task Force 53 (Attack Force)   R/Adm Harry W. Hill
Task Force 54 (Gunfire & Covering Force)   R/Adm Bertram J. Rogers
Task Force 56 (Expeditionary Troops)   LtGen Holland M. Smith
Task Group 56-1 (Landing Force)   MajGen Harry Schmidt
Task Force 58 (Fast Carrier Force – 5th Fleet)   V/Adm Marc A. Mitscher
Task Force 93 (Strategic Air Force –
  Pacific Ocean Area)   LtGen Hillard F. Harmon
Task Force 94 (Forward Area – Central Pacific)   V/Adm John H. Hoover

**Aerial view of Mount Suribachi
from the west in March, 2000.
(Taro Kuribayashi)**

APPENDIX NO. 2

JAPANESE COMMAND AND STAFF LIST

Commander in Chief	LtGen Tadamichi Kuribayashi
Chief of Staff	Col Tadashi Takaishi

ARMY UNITS

109th Division	LtGen Tadamichi Kuribayashi
145th Infantry Regiment	Col Masuo Ikeda
17th Mixed Infantry Regiment	Maj Tamachi Fujiwara
26th Tank Regiment	LtCol (Baron) Takeichi Nishi
2nd Mixed Brigade	MajGen Sadasue Senda
Brigade Artillery	Col Chosaku Kaido
Army Rocket Unit	Capt Yoshio Yokoyama

NAVY UNITS

Commanding Officer	R/Adm Toshinosuke Ichimaru
Naval Guard Force	Capt Samaji Inouye
125th Naval Anti-Aircraft Defense Unit	Lt Tamura
132nd Naval Anti-Aircraft Defense Unit	En Okumura
141st Naval Anti-Aircraft Defense Unit	Lt Doi
149th Naval Anti-Aircraft Defense Unit	Not known
Operations.	Comm Takeji Mase
Communications	LtComm Shigeru Arioka
Engineering	LtComm Narimasa Okada
Supply	LtComm Okazaki
Suribachi Commander	Capt Kanehiko Atsuchi

Total number of Japanese forces on Iwo Jima – February 19, 1945 (D-Day). – 21060.

Associated Press photographer Joe Rosenthal with his Speed Graphic camera stands atop Mount Suribachi minutes after taking the picture that was to make him famous. (USMC)

APPENDIX NO. 3

FLAGS OVER SURIBACHI

The Second World War produced many outstanding photographs – Cecil Beaton's picture of the dome of St Paul's Cathedral surrounded by a ring of fire during the London Blitz, the mushroom cloud over Hiroshima, Gen Douglas MacArthur wading ashore in the Philippines, and the horrific pits full of emaciated bodies at Belsen concentration camp to name a few – but none of them achieved the fame of Joe Rosenthal's picture of US Marines raising the flag on the summit of Mount Suribachi.

When it was first seen in America it became an instant sensation and lent itself to an issue of three-cent stamps that had the largest sale in history. A painting was used for the 7th War loan drive that raised $220,000,000, it appeared on 3,500,000 posters, and 175,000 car cards, was portrayed in films, re-enacted by gymnasts, and a float won first prize in the Rose Bowl Parade. The greatest accolade was the 100-ton bronze statue by Felix de Weldon that stands near the northern end of Arlington National Cemetery in Washington, DC, as a memorial to the United States Marine Corps.

Because of its outstanding composition and the fact that it was the second flag to be raised that day, there has always been speculation that the picture was posed, a view compounded by many books and magazine articles over the years. In correspondence with the author, Joe Rosenthal gives the true story of the events of that day and clears up the misconceptions for good.

On the February 23, Joe boarded an ICT along with Bill Hippie, a magazine correspondent, and landed near Mount Suribachi where the boatswain told them that a patrol was going up Suribachi with a flag. They went to the 28th Regiment command post and learned that a 40-man detachment had already left following two patrols that had reached the top at 0940hrs. At the command post were Bob Campbell, a combat photographer, and Sgt Bill Genaust, a cine photographer (killed nine days later at Hill 362); and Rosenthal, Genaust and Campbell started the tough climb, stopping occasionally while Marines dealt with enemy troops holed up in caves.

About half way up they met four Marines coming down. One was Lou Lowery, a photographer for *Leatherneck*, the Marine Corps magazine, who told them that a flag had been raised on the summit and that he had photographed the event. Joe was in two minds whether to continue but decided to press on and take a picture anyway. Reaching the top of the volcano, he saw the flag flying and also saw a group of men dragging a long iron pipe and holding another neatly folded flag. "What are you doing?" he asked. "We're going to put up this bigger flag and keep the other as a souvenir," they said. This second flag came from IST 779 which was beached at the base of Suribachi. Ensign Alan Wood who was aboard told the author: "A dirty, dusty, battle-worn Marine (2nd Lt Albert Tuttle) asked for a flag. It was one that had been salvaged from a supply depot at Pearl Harbor. I hadn't the slightest idea that one day it would become the symbol of one of the war's bloodiest battlefields."

Rosenthal toyed with the idea of a shot showing the first flag coming down and the second one going up, but left that to Campbell and concentrated on a picture of the second flag being raised. He moved back but the sloping ground masked his view and he had to build a platform of sandbags and

Pvt Robert Campbell took this photograph of the first flag being lowered as the second flag was raised. Rosenthal and Genaust were standing a few yards to his left. (USMC)

Joe Rosenthal assembled a group of Marines for a posed shot after taking his famous flag raising picture. It was this that was to start the rumours that his famous picture was "posed." (USMC)

stones (he is only 5ft 5in tall). With Genaust standing on his right, he saw the men start to raise the flag and shouted, "There she goes," and swung his camera and caught the scene. He also took pictures of a group of Marines under the flag waving and cheering before he and Campbell made their way back to the 28th Regiment command post.

Back on the USS *Eldorado*, he wrote captions for the day's pictures and handed them in to go on the daily mail plane to Guam. When his picture reached the United States via radiophoto it was an immediate sensation. Ironically, Joe was not to see it for another nine days when he returned to Guam where he was congratulated by a group of correspondents. "It's a great picture," they said. "Did you pose it?" "Sure," he said – he thought that they were referring to the shot with the waving and cheering Marines, but then someone showed him the picture. "Pose that one?" "Gee," I said. "That's good alright, but I didn't pose that one." It was here that the first misunderstandings about the picture started. Someone heard him say that he had posed a picture and wrote that the shot was a phoney and that Rosenthal had posed it.

Joe Rosenthal's life was completely changed by that photo. He was recalled to America by Associated Press where he became a celebrity, got a raise in salary, was awarded the Pulitzer Prize, and met President Harry Truman. Speaking engagements followed, at one of which he was bizarrely introduced as "Mr. Joe Rosenberg who raised the flag at Okinawa."

The accusations of a posed photograph have been a sore point since the end of the war as the old misconceptions continued to re-appear in books and magazines over the years. The "posed" myth is easily discounted by looking at Bill Genaust's five-second cine film taken at the same time which shows one frame identical to Rosenthal's photograph. Joe Rosenthal's final words on the subject are: "I can best sum up what I feel by saying that of all the elements that went into the making of this picture, the part I played was the least important. To get that flag up there, America's fighting men had to die on that island and on other islands, and off the shore, and in the air. What difference does it make who took the picture? I took it, but the Marines took Iwo Jima."

The six flag raisers in the picture are all now deceased. They were from left to right: Pfc Ira Hayes, Pfc Franklin Sousley, Sgt Michael Strank, Pharmacist's Mate 2nd Class John H. Bradley, Pfc Rene A. Gagnon and Cpl Harlon H. Block (Sousley, Strank and Block were all killed on Iwo Jima). Both flags now hang in the Marine Corps Historical Center in Washington, DC.

RIGHT **Aerial picture of the Marine Corps Memorial on the day of the dedication ceremony, November 10, 1954. The ceremony was conducted by President Dwight D. Eisenhower accompanied by Vice President Richard Nixon and the then Commandant of the Marine Corps, General Lemuel C. Shepherd, Jr. (USMC)**

APPENDIX NO. 4

THE MARINE CORPS MEMORIAL

Directly inspired by Joe Rosenthal's famous Iwo Jima photograph, a Memorial to the United States Marine Corps was erected at Arlington National Cemetery in Washington, DC, in 1954. The sculptor, Felix de Weldon, chose the Iwo Jima image as the Marine Corps symbol most familiar to the American public although the Memorial of course represents the nation's tribute to the dead of the Corps since its formation in 1775. Three years in the making, the figures are 32ft high and stand on a Swedish granite base surrounded by polished black granite blocks listing the names and dates of all major Marine Corps engagements since the Corps was founded. Also engraved on the base is Adm Chester Nimitz's famous tribute to the Marines of Iwo Jima: "Uncommon Valor was a Common Virtue."

The Memorial was official dedicated on November 10, 1954, by President Dwight D. Eisenhower, accompanied by Vice President Richard Nixon and the then Commandant of the Marine Corps, Gen Lemuel C. Shepherd, Jr. Also present at the ceremony were the three surviving flag raisers from Rosenthal's picture, John H. Bradley, Ira Hayes and Rene A. Gagnon. Surprisingly, Rosenthal's name was not mentioned on the monument and it was many years before it was acknowledged that the statue was based on his photograph and a plaque was added to the base.

Pharmacist's Mate 2nd Class John H. Bradley (US Navy) seldom spoke of his part in the flag raising, even to his family, and lived a quiet post-war life in his home town of Antigo, Wisconsin. The longest surviving member of the six who raised the second flag on Mount Suribachi, he died aged 70 in January 1994.

Corporal Ira H. Hayes, a Pima Indian from the Gila River Reservation in Arizona, enlisted in the Corps in 1942 as a member of the Parachute Regiment. When this unit was disbanded in 1944 he was transferred to the 5th Division with which he served at Iwo Jima. Ordered back to the US after the flag raising to promote a War Bond selling tour, he found the publicity overwhelming and welcomed the return to his unit. In later life he had major problems with alcoholism and died aged 32 in 1955 and is buried in Arlington National Cemetery.

Rene Gagnon, a 5th Division Marine, was also co-opted to the Treasury Department to promote the 7th War Loan Drive and, after he returned to his unit, served with the occupation forces in China until his discharge in 1946. He died in 1979 and was buried in Manchester, New Hampshire. In 1981 at the request of his widow he was re-interred in Arlington Cemetery.

This 100-ton bronze statue designed by Felix de Weldon is the memorial to the United States Marine Corps at Arlington National Cemetery in Washington, DC. (USMC)

All three survivors had posed for de Weldon who modeled their faces in clay. Photographs of the deceased flag raisers were used to depict their likenesses. The castings of the figures took almost three years to complete and were made at the Bedi-Rassy Art Foundry in Brooklyn, New York.

The Monument was funded by US Marines, Reservists, friends of the Marine Corps and members of the Naval Service at a cost of $850,000 – no public funds were used. Now one of Washington's major tourist attractions and certainly the most striking War Memorial in the capital, the monument has stood for over four decades in tribute to the Corps.

A major controversy arose recently when the US Air Force attempted to secure an area near the Memorial for their own monument. It was rightly judged that another large structure so close to this one would be obtrusive and detract from the Marine Corps Memorial. After much inter-service and political in-fighting, the Air Force were obliged to find a location elsewhere on the Arlington site.

LEFT **The three surviving flag raisers were invited to the ceremony. They are, from left to right, John H. Bradley, Ira Hayes and Rene A. Gagnon. All are now deceased. (USMC)**

OPPOSITE **This dramatic shot from the rear of a landing craft shows the chaos into which the Marines were deposited – volcanic ash up to their ankles, enemy pillboxes and bunkers straight ahead, and more troops arriving every five minutes. (National Archives)**

APPENDIX NO.5

THE MEDAL OF HONOR – UNCOMMON VALOR

The United States' highest decoration, the Medal of Honor, was awarded to 27 combatants at Iwo Jima, a figure that represents a third of the total number of awards to members of the United States Marine Corps during the whole of World War II. Admiral Chester Nimitz's words: "Among the Americans who served on Iwo Jima, uncommon valor was a common virtue," could not have been more appropriate.

Cpl CHARLES J.BERRY – *1st Battalion 26th Regiment 5th Division* (Posthumous)
On the night of March 3, Berry and two other riflemen were in a foxhole close to Nishi Ridge. A group of Japanese made an infiltration and lobbed a hand grenade into the foxhole whereupon Berry immediately threw himself on to it and was killed instantly, saving the lives of his comrades.

Pfc WILLIAM CADDY – *3rd Battalion 26th Regiment 5th Division* (Posthumous)
North of Airfield No. 3, a Japanese sniper had Caddy and his two companions pinned down for two hours in a shell hole. Around 1600hrs one of the Marines scrambled to the edge of the hole to try to locate the enemy but was spotted. The sniper threw a hand grenade, and Caddy threw himself onto it and took the full blast in his chest and stomach, dying immediately.

LtCol JUSTICE M. CHAMBERS – *3rd Battalion 25th Regiment 4th Division*
At 38, "Jumpin' Joe" Chambers was one of the old men of the battle. Determined to take "Charlie Dog Ridge," he called in a salvo of rockets and rushed to the head of his men in a wild charge towards the summit, but was hit in the chest by a burst of machine gun fire and was dragged back to his observation post. After a long convalescence in America he received his medal from President Truman at the White House.

On the fourth day of the battle the 21st Regiment were faced with a stubborn complex of bunkers and anti-tank guns adjoining Airfield No 2 in the center of the island. Maj Houser called upon 21-year-old Cpl Hershel Williams, the last of his flamethrowers, to go forward escorted by riflemen. With complete disregard for his own safety, Williams moved from one position to another, burning out bunkers and strongpoints, until the way ahead had been cleared. He was the first 3rd Division Marine on Iwo Jima to be awarded the Medal of Honor.

Sgt DARRELL S. COLE – *1st Battalion 23rd Regiment 4th Division* (Posthumous)
Storming the beaches on D-Day, Cole's platoon came under very heavy fire from pillboxes on Yellow
Beaches 1 and 2. Armed with hand grenades and a .45cal pistol he silenced six positions, returning to
his lines twice for more ammunition before being killed by an enemy grenade that exploded at his feet.

Capt ROBERT H. DUNLAP – *1st Battalion 26th Regiment 5th Division*
Dunlap's company were pinned down near Airfield No. 1 under a hail of mortar fire. Grabbing a field
telephone he advanced to an isolated position only 50yds (46m) from the enemy and for the next
48 hours called in devastating fire on the Japanese positions from various directions, playing a
significant role in clearing the western section of the island.

Sgt ROSS F. GRAY – *1st Battalion 25th Regiment 4th Division*
When his platoon became bogged down in fighting around Airfield No. 2, Gray grabbed a satchel
charge and silenced the nearest emplacement. In short order he repeated the process until all six
adjacent positions lay silent and the way was clear for an advance. Later in the day Gray cleared a
path through a dangerous minefield single-handedly.

Sgt WILLIAM G. HARRELL – *1st Battalion 28th Regiment 5th Division*
Manning a front line foxhole near Nishi Ridge, Sgt Harrell and Pfc Carter were attacked by nighttime
infiltrators. Four of them were swiftly disposed of before a hand grenade was thrown into the position
and almost blew off Harrell's left hand and caused other serious injuries. Carter's gun had jammed and
he left to get another. Meanwhile two more Japanese charged into the foxhole, one placed a grenade
next to Harrell and attempted to leave. Harrell shot him with his pistol and lobbed the grenade out, but
it exploded blowing off his right hand. The indomitable sergeant was evacuated next morning and after
the war, with the aid of mechanical hands, became a rancher in his native Texas.

Lt RUFUS G. HERRING – *USNR LGI(G) 449*
The first of Iwo Jima's medal winners, Herring was the captain of Gunboat 449 which was laying down
a carpet of rockets in support of frogmen two days before D-Day. A direct hit from Japanese artillery
killed 12 of the crew and seriously wounded Herring. Bleeding profusely he struggled for thirty minutes
to steer his vessel and wounded crew away from the enemy barrage and alongside the destroyed
USS *Terror*, remaining propped up by empty shell cases until all of his men had been evacuated.

Pfc DOUGLAS T. JACOBSON – *3rd Battalion 23rd Regiment 4th Division*
Battling to take Hill 382, 19 year old Jacobson seized a bazooka and began to wage his own war on
the enemy. For thirty minutes he ran from blockhouse to blockhouse, blasting each one in turn until
sixteen positions fell silent and 75 of the enemy lay dead, opening up a gap for his company to reach
the top of the hill. Using a bazooka is a two-man operation, but Jacobson achieved his remarkable
feat alone.

90

The twelve LCI gunboats
supporting the activities of the
Navy frogmen came in for lethal
enemy gunfire. Made largely of
wood, the frail craft were easy
targets for Japanese gunners
who had had months to practice.
Here a crewman lies dead
among the spent ammunition
on the vessel. (US Navy)

FAR, RIGHT **Douglas Jacobson, seen here at an Iwo Jima reunion in Wichita Falls, Texas, in March, 2000, proudly displays his Medal of Honor. (Author)**

RIGHT **Mr. Taro Kuribayashi, son of the Japanese commander of Iwo Jima, stands beside the 5th Division memorial. Mr. Kuribayashi is a frequent visitor to the island and actively promotes American–Japanese reconciliation. (Taro Kuribayashi)**

Sgt JOSEPH R. JULIAN – *1st Battalion 27th Regiment 5th Division* (Posthumous)
In vicious fighting around Kitano Point on the 18th day of the battle, Julian silenced four enemy emplacements and a machine gun nest. Dashing back to his lines he collected demolition charges and a bazooka and once more charged the enemy, this time destroying four more strongpoints before being killed by a burst of machine gun fire.

Pfc JAMES D. LaBELLE – *2nd Battalion 27th Regiment 5th Division* (Posthumous)
It seems that LaBelle was destined to die on Iwo Jima. On D-Day he missed death by inches when three companions were mown down by machine gun fire; three days later he was the only one unhurt when a grenade landed in a shell hole he was sharing with four other Marines; and on day ten his best friend died at his side near Nishi Ridge. While they were standing behind an outcrop of boulders with two friends, a solitary Japanese soldier lobbed a grenade into their midst. Shouting a warning, Labelle threw himself on the grenade saving the lives of the others.

2nd Lt JOHN H. LEIMS – *1st Battalion 9th Regiment 3rd Division*
Attacking Hill 362C, east of Cushman's Pocket, Leims and his company were cut off. He personally advanced and laid telephone lines across an exposed expanse of fire-swept terrain. Later, learning that several casualties were still behind enemy lines, he made two trips under heavy fire to bring back his wounded.

Pfc JACKLYN H. LUCAS – *1st Battalion 26th Regiment 5th Division*
A born rebel, Lucas had enlisted in the Corps when he was only 14; now at 17 he was wanted by the Military Police in Hawaii for being AWOL. On D+1 near Airfield No. 1 he was one of three men pinned down by enemy fire. When grenades fell among them he grabbed one and smothered it with his body and then grabbed a second and pulled it underneath him. Miraculously he survived the blasts and after spending months in hospital recovered with only a partially paralysed arm.

1st Lt JACK LUMMUS – *2nd Battalion 27th Regiment 5th Division* (Posthumous)
Determined to keep up the momentum while attacking a complex of enemy caves and bunkers near Kitano Point, Lummus, a 29 year old ex-professional football star from Texas, spearheaded an attack and was soon blown to the ground by a grenade. Jumping to his feet, he attacked the position to his front killing the occupants. Waving his men forward for another charge, he stepped on a mine and both legs were blown off. As the debris settled, his men were horrified to see him upright on his stumps still urging them forward. He died several hours later in a field hospital

1st Lt HARRY L. MARTIN – *5th Pioneer Battalion* (Posthumous)
Before dawn on the March 26, between 200 and 300 Japanese troops, the remnants of Gen Kuribayashi's command, launched a massed attack against a rest area occupied by aircrews, Seabees and other non-combat troops west of Airfield No. 2. Martin immediately formed a defense line manned mainly by Black troops and held many of the enemy in check. He recovered a number of wounded and attacked a machine gun position killing four of the enemy before being seriously wounded by a grenade. As dawn revealed the carnage, the body of Martin was recovered from among the hundreds strewn around the camp.

Capt JOSEPH J. McCARTHY – *2nd Battalion 24th Regiment 4th Division*
Another "Jumpin' Joe", 33 year old McCarthy, rallying his men on the approach to Airfield No. 2, filled bags with grenades, mustered a three-man flamethrower team, and headed for the enemy yelling: "Let's get the bastards before they get us." Thrusting grenades through the firing vents, he personally silenced four pillboxes allowing his company to advance.

Pvt GEORGE PHILLIPS – *2nd Battalion 28th Regiment 5th Division.* (Posthumous)
On the very day that Iwo Jima was officially declared "secure," Pfc Phillips, an 18 year old replacement who had only landed on the island two days earlier, threw himself onto a grenade and died instantly, saving the lives of the three companions that he barely knew.

Pharmacist's Mate 1st Class FRANCIS PIERCE, Jr. – *2nd Battalion 24th Regiment 4th Division*
Corpsman Pierce and a party of stretcher-bearers were ambushed while evacuating wounded on March 15. He engaged the enemy with rifle fire and carried a wounded Marine to safety, returning for another while under constant fire from Japanese snipers. Badly wounded the following day, he refused aid and continued to minister to casualties until he collapsed. Pierce's actions were typical of Iwo Jima's Corpsmen, and show why they were held in such high regard by the Marines.

Pfc DONALD J. RUHL – *2nd Battalion 28th Regiment 5th Division* (Posthumous)
21 year old Ruhl showed conspicuous gallantry from the day that he landed on Iwo Jima. On D-Day he killed nine of the enemy while charging a blockhouse. The following morning he dragged a wounded Marine to safety across 40yds (37m) of ground swept by heavy fire and later occupied an enemy gun emplacement and secured it overnight to prevent the enemy from re-occupying it. He met his death on D+2 when he and his platoon sergeant were in a camouflaged bunker bringing fire to bear on the enemy. A grenade landed between the pair, and without a thought for his own safety he threw himself upon it to protect his companion.

Pvt FRANKLIN E. SIGLER – *2nd Battalion 26th Regiment 5th Division*
In the final stage of the battle in Death Valley, Sigler took command of his leaderless squad and led an attack against a gun emplacement that was causing chaos among the 2nd Battalion. In the face of murderous fire he silenced the position with hand grenades, killing the entire enemy crew, but was severely wounded by fire from nearby caves. Continuing the attack, he sealed several caves before withdrawing to his lines. Refusing medical treatment, he carried three wounded Marines to safety and continued to direct rocket and machine gun fire at the enemy until ordered to the rear for medical treatment.

Cpl TONY STEIN – *1st Battalion 28th Regiment 5th Division*
During the advance across the island at the base of Mount Suribachi on D-Day, Stein, armed with an improvised aircraft .50cal machine gun that he called his "stinger," attacked five enemy positions killing at least 20 of the enemy. When his ammunition ran out he made repeated trips to the beach for more, carrying a wounded marine back each time. Although wounded by shrapnel, he continued to fight, supervising the withdrawal of his platoon although having his "stinger" twice shot from his hands. Stein was killed near Hill 362A later in the battle, never knowing of his citation.

Gunnery Sgt WILLIAM G. WALSH – *3rd Battalion 27th Regiment 5th Division* (Posthumous)
During the attack on Hill 362A, Walsh led his platoon to the summit in the face of heavy enemy fire, but his success was short lived when they were forced to withdraw under devastating machine gun fire from three enemy positions. Undeterred, Walsh mounted a counterattack, again reaching the top where the six men in his squad took cover in a trench. The Japanese retaliated by lobbing hand grenades and when one fell in their midst Walsh threw himself upon it and died instantly.

Pvt WILSON D. WATSON – *2nd Battalion 9th Regiment 3rd Division*
Two hills, codenamed Peter and Oboe, near Airfield No. 2 were formidable stumbling blocks for the

Herschel "Woody" Williams still attends Iwo Jima reunions and is one of the diminishing number of Iwo Jima Medal of Honor recipients. (Author)

RIGHT **Here seen in the setting sun, the Memorial is one of Washington's most striking images and a very popular tourist attraction. (USMC)**

3rd Division. Watson was the first man atop Hill Oboe, having silenced a bunker and a machine gun nest on the way. Aided by only one other Marine, he staved off repeated enemy attacks for thirty minutes until reinforcements arrived in support. Pressing forward, he destroyed another bunker and was attacking a second when he was wounded by mortar fire and had to be evacuated for treatment. In two days he had killed over 90 of the enemy and played a major role in the reduction of these key positions.

Pharmacist's Mate 2nd Class GEORGE E. WHALEN – *2nd Battalion 26th Regiment 5th Division*
Another of Iwo's gallant Corpsmen, Whalen was wounded on February 26, but continued tending the injured despite intense enemy fire. Wounded again on March 3, he refused aid and was wounded for a third time but crawled among the casualties to administer aid until he had to be carried to the rear for urgent treatment. When evacuated, Whalen had been treating wounded Marines non-stop for five days and nights.

Cpl HERSHEL W. WILLIAMS – *1st Battalion 21st Regiment 3rd Division*
Confronted with a complex of bunkers and anti-tank guns adjoining Airfield No. 2, Maj Robert Houser called upon 21 year old Williams, the last of his flamethrowers. Escorted by riflemen, he incinerated the occupants of the first pillbox and a group of Japanese troops who attempted to shoot him down. Moving from one position to another he burned out bunkers and pillboxes and in four hours had cleared the way for his regiment to move forward. Williams was the first 3rd Division Marine on Iwo Jima to win the Medal of Honor.

Pharmacist's Mate 3rd Class JACK WILLIAMS – *3rd Battalion 28th Regiment 5th Division*
(Posthumous)
Williams, a 21-year-old from Harrison, Arkansas, added to the prestige of Iwo's Corpsmen on March 20. Under heavy fire he went to aid a wounded Marine, screening him from enemy fire with his own body while attending to his wounds. Inevitably he was wounded himself, receiving gunshots to the abdomen and groin, but continued treating his patient before attending to his own injuries. He then moved on to a second casualty and although bleeding profusely, administered aid before attempting to return to the rear but was killed by an enemy sniper.

Pharmacist's Mate 1st Class JOHN H. WILLIS – *3rd Battalion 27th Regiment 5th Division*
(Posthumous)
Willis had been tending the wounded all day around Hill 362 on February 28 until he was wounded by shrapnel and was ordered to the rear for treatment. Within hours he was back with the troops attending a seriously wounded Marine in a shell hole. With his rifle stuck in the ground, he was administering plasma when a grenade rolled down beside him. He threw it out, but seven more followed in rapid succession and each was quickly thrown out until the last one exploded in his hand killing him instantly.

INDEX

COMPANION SERIES FROM OSPREY

MEN-AT-ARMS

An unrivalled source of information on the organization, uniforms and equipment of the world's fighting men, past and present. The series covers hundreds of subjects spanning 5,000 years of history. Each 48-page book includes concise texts packed with specific information, some 40 photos, maps and diagrams, and eight color plates of uniformed figures.

ELITE

Detailed information on the uniforms and insignia of the world's most famous military forces. Each 64-page book contains some 50 photographs and diagrams, and 12 pages of full-color artwork.

NEW VANGUARD

Comprehensive histories of the design, development and operational use of the world's armored vehicles and artillery. Each 48-page book contains eight pages of full-color artwork including a detailed cutaway.

WARRIOR

Definitive analysis of the armor, weapons, tactics and motivation of the fighting men of history. Each 64-page book contains cutaways and exploded artwork of the warrior's weapons and armor.

ORDER OF BATTLE

The most detailed information ever published on the units that fought history's great battles. Each 96-page book contains comprehensive organization diagrams supported by ultra-detailed color maps. Each title also includes a large fold-out base map.

AIRCRAFT OF THE ACES

Focuses exclusively on the elite pilots of major air campaigns, and includes unique interviews with surviving aces sourced specifically for each volume. Each 96-page volume contains up to 40 specially commissioned artworks, unit listings, new scale plans and the best archival photography available.

COMBAT AIRCRAFT

Technical information from the world's leading aviation writers on the aircraft types flown. Each 96-page volume contains up to 40 specially commissioned artworks, unit listings, new scale plans and the best archival photography available.